Leadership Development Guide

*A Competency-Based Approach
to Individual Growth and Organizational Effectiveness*

*Introducing the **Leadership Role Continuum**:
focus on the leadership competencies most important
to your current or desired role*

*With **behavioral examples**
for each leadership competency*

Peter A. Stinson, M.A., M.Ed.
Editor

Leadership Development Guide
A Competency-Based Approach
to Individual Growth and Organizational Effectiveness

20190925

ISBN: 9781070973623

===========
Deer Hollow Way
Fairfax, Virginia
===========

The Leadership Development Guide
is dedicated to those throughout my career
who have encouraged my professional development:
too numerous to name, spanning
decades upon decades,
and always helping me find the way.

May I, in turn, encourage you
with your professional development;
please let this little guide help you
as you move deliberately through your career.

My thanks to the Wolfpack
for their watchful support during trying times;
we are on the other side, and I am with you still.

No one journeys through life alone.

Table of Contents

Preface

Why care about leadership competencies? This is a great question. I recently read Marcus Buckingham and Ashley Goodall's cutting edge book *Nine Lies About Work*; they eviscerate the use of leadership competencies. Frankly, that was a bit of a bummer since I'd been working on this guide. I agree, however, that when leadership competencies are used for evil, we should look for other options.

Here's where I stand. Leadership competencies are a decent model; the model captures the skills, knowledge, abilities, and experiences necessary to do the job. The model, and the competencies, are not perfect. I don't expect you to excel in more than one or two. I don't. We have things we do well. We have things we don't do well. I expect that you can be proficient in all of the leadership competencies. Or, you can use aids or supports to be proficient. You'll exceed at some; hopefully, we will be proficient in all.

I find the competency model to be helpful. Used as a developmental tool, it can help an individual see where they are strong and where they could use some improvement. Used as a mandatory gauge or evaluation criteria, it can be detrimental to the entire organization.

Use this leadership development guide in good health. Know that the purpose here is not to hold employees to an impossible standard, but to create a system wherein employees can grow and develop and the organization has a plan for leadership succession.

Join me on this great journey. Come with me, and touch the future.

Introduction

Even the most casual trip requires us to choose a destination, consult a map, and plan our journey. Your career, and the careers of those around you, are the same. It's a journey; a map is helpful. I will agree that unlike a destination, for our careers we frequently don't land where we think we are going. When I was just starting out, I didn't even know the field of organizational development existed, and it certainly didn't exist in the same way it does today.

This leadership development guide will provide you some guidance on your leadership journey. And, I would note, that all of us are leaders. The skills and competencies necessary to be a good leader are the skills and competencies necessary to thrive and excel in our lives.

Within this guide, you will be introduced to several models. One of these models is a leadership role continuum which outlines the leadership continuum and the leadership competencies needed to succeed in the role. This guide also provides the details to identify and develop the competencies needed at each stop along the continuum. This continuum is, in a sense, a map providing guidance for advancing from point A to point B, from one one role to another.

Today's organizations will not succeed without skilled leaders who can move an organization forward in turbulent times. Employees in every organization are entrusted to do work, to support the mission of the organization, and to create the desired organizational outcomes. As such, all employees exhibit leadership skills on a daily basis, whether through their interactions with stakeholders or with coworkers. Individual employee leadership is underscored by initiative, competence, and the desire to achieve excellence. This individual leadership is the foundation for meeting goals and creating desired outcomes for our stakeholders.

To meet the mission and create the desired outcomes, every organization needs skilled leaders at the supervisory, management, and executive levels. Recent research by Marcus

Buckingham and Ashley Goodall, published in *Nine Lies About Work* (Harvard Business Review Press, 2019), finds that the role of team leader has the greatest impact on employee engagement and organizational excellence. These leaders define and communicate expectations, roles, and responsibilities to employees, provide resources for employee development, and recognize employee accomplishments. And, these leaders must be worthy of trust. Those with strong leadership skills inspire employees to meet the challenges of today's fast-paced, ever-changing regulatory world.

A leader...
Leads by example
Strives to make a positive difference
Inspires and encourages
Respects others
Provides support
Recognizes the contributions of others

What Makes a Leader? When will it my turn?

Everyone can be a leader, regardless of official position. I might go so far to say that all of are in positions to demonstrate leadership. Whether or not we are designated as leaders because of our position, it is the responsibility of each employee to take ownership in developing leadership competencies. This guide lays out a leadership competency development framework and the ways an employee can acquire those leadership skills.

Every organization experiences employee "churn." People go. In some organizations, such as the federal government, projections are that high percentages of leaders will continue to leave the civil service workforce. Other organizations are in a similar boat. This continued attrition will create opportunities for others to apply for vacated leadership positions.

Employees who invest time and energy in developing leadership competencies will be better prepared to compete for positions. Those who are willing to relocate will find more leadership positions available in their interest area. While developing your leadership skills will not guarantee you a position, those developmental efforts will increase your marketability when you do apply for positions. So, plan your journey, assess your progress, and use the developmental opportunities and support structures available.

How to Use the Toolkit and Roadmap

What are the goals of this guide? The goals of this guide are three-fold:
- To help create workplaces where employees and supervisors both take responsibility for leadership development
- To improve the leadership skills of all employees
- To help organizations meet succession planning needs.

*Use this guide to move
from contemplating development
to taking action.*

Steps for Using This Guide

While there's not a "right" or "wrong" way to use this guide, please allow me to offer a few suggestions.

Read Chapters 1 and 2 first. (Well, after you're finished with the Introduction. Please do keep reading here.) Chapter 1 covers key concepts and Chapter 2 will lead you through the seven step developmental journey for planning and completing your leadership voyage.

Look at Chapters 3 through 7. Thumb through the chapter that applies to your current position on the leadership role continuum. I know, more than one role likely applies to you. Thumb through both. Or all. You are both an employee and a manager; you are an employee, a team lead, and a supervisor; you are in executive, and you also have subordinates who you supervise. Don't read in depth; you're only scrolling pages now. Five roles are on the leadership role continuum. They are employee, team leaders/project manager, supervisor, manager, and executive.

Pick the chapter for the current role you want to focus on now. One chapter. You can't focus on a twenty things at a time. Pick one. It's a bit of a WAG, but you're in for the long hall; you can do them all over time if you'd like.

Work through the seven developmental steps from Chapter 2 fore the role you've chosen. Remember, you'll likely never be phenomenal in all of the competencies. Anyone who asks otherwise isn't thinking. Lionel Messi, an awesome soccer player, relies on his left foot. All the time. When he needs to do something fantastic, it's with his left foot. Always. He has a strength and he uses it. Can he kick with his right foot? Sure. But his strength, what he's really good at, is using his left foot. He's proficient with his right. You want to get to the same place: able to smash the competencies that are your talent, your strength, and to be proficient in all the rest.

Chapter 1:
The Continuum for Leadership Development

To develop our leadership skills, we need to know our destination, assess our current proficiency level, and use available learning resources and support structures. The key components of leadership development are:

- Leadership competencies as learning goals
- Assessment and feedback
- Continuous learning opportunities
- Mentoring

Leadership competencies as learning goals. The leadership continuum lists the competencies needed for successful performance within each role. Focus, first, on developing the competencies important for where you are; next, work on the competencies for the where you want to be.

Assessment and feedback. There are a variety of assessment tools to identify strengths, personal styles, and related developmental needs. Your organization may offer some of them. You can also find some assessment tools online, such as the free assessment tools developed by FranklinCovey at https://assessments.franklincovey.com/. Use the results of the assessments to create your developmental plan.

Continuous learning opportunities. You're not going anywhere unless you are learning. Keep your mind sharp. Keep your skills up to snuff. Learn. We learn in a number of situations, different learning approaches to best meet each employee's learning style and developmental needs. You will find opportunities in learning through classroom training, e-learning, developmental assignments, and self-directed activities. Use these learning approaches to develop the leadership competencies you targeted.

Mentoring. Mentoring, as defined by the University of Cambridge, is a "system of semi-structured guidance whereby one person shares their knowledge, skills and experience to assist others to progress in their own lives and careers." Use a mentoring relationship, and other supportive services in one-on-one and team settings. Use these mentoring and supportive services to help plan your goals, sustain your progress, and transfer learning back to the job. (For more information about mentoring, and to see how a world-class university uses mentoring to drive learning and research, see https://www.ppd.admin.cam.ac.uk/professional-development/mentoring-university-cambridge)

What is a Leadership Competency?

A competency is an observable, measurable pattern of knowledge, skills, abilities, or characteristics an individual needs for effective or superior performance in a job. A competency can be measured against agreed-upon standards and can be improved through learning and practice. Effective leaders need both the technical expertise inherent for a particular job and the leadership competencies appropriate for the leadership level of the position (Employee, Project Manager/Team Leader, Supervisor, Manager, and Executive).

This guide will assist you with identifying the leadership competencies you need for each role and planning learning experiences to attain those leadership competencies. Consult people within your organization for information on the technical expertise needed for a specific position and suggestions for their development. Use LinkedIn, or other work-focused social media platforms to seek input for development.

The Leadership Role Continuum illustrates how leadership is developed along the continuum. Each role on the continuum lists the competencies needed at that level and the common learning experiences that can be used to attain skills for that leadership role.

Leadership Role Continuum

This leadership role continuum illustrates a model of building leadership capacity. For each role on the continuum, the primary competencies needed at that level, and the common learning experiences that can be used to attain the skills for that role, are noted. The continuum provides a progressive nature of the leadership through the role levels.

Yes, that's not how life is. Life isn't an orderly progression of steps. But the model is helpful. I've never met a model I didn't like. All models are useful. Most are flawed in some way. Same for this model: flawed and useful.

Each part of the continuum focuses on the leadership competencies most critical for that role, building on the other roles in the continuum.

Leadership Role Continuum

All Employees --> Team Leader --> Supervisor --> Manager --> Executive

---

Role: **All Employees**

Primary focus:
Managing and Leading Yourself

Core Competencies:
- Continual Learning
- Customer Service
- Flexibility
- Integrity/Honesty
- Interpersonal Skills
- Oral Communication
- Problem Solving
- Resilience
- Written Communication
- Cross-Cultural Interactions

Learning Experiences:
- Develop a learning contract/individual development plan with supervisor
- Have a mentor/be a mentor
- Engage in some cross training within program
- Volunteer for collateral duty assignments and/or specific projects
- Join and become active in outside professional organizations
- Participate in external education and training courses
- Complete self-study online courses
- Engage in self-directed learning through books, magazines, podcasts, "Ted" talks, tapes and/or seminars

Role: Team Leader/Project Manager

Primary focus:
Leading Teams and Managing Projects

Core Competencies:
- Decisiveness
- Influencing/Negotiating
- Team Building
- Technical Credibility

Learning Experiences:
- Complete a 360° assessment and obtain/review results
- Have a mentor/be a mentor
- Participate in a detail within your organization or, even, in a different organization
- Visit program sites/field/headquarters
- Serve as a member of an organization-wide special project team
- Develop a development plan based on 360° feedback
- Complete a formal Project Management training
- Participate in external education and training courses
- Complete self-study online courses
- Engage in self-directed learning through books, podcasts, tapes, seminars, etc.

Role: **Supervisor**

Primary focus:
Leading People

Core Competencies:
- Accountability
- Conflict Management
- Developing Others
- Human Capital Management
- Leveraging Diversity

Learning Experiences:
- Complete a 360°assessment and obtain/review results
- Have a mentor/be a mentor
- Participate in a detail within the larger organization
- Serve as a representative on a company/program/ organization/agency/department committee
- Develop a development plan based on 360° feedback
- Complete a formal supervisory training program
- Complete self-study online courses
- Within first year as new supervisor, conduct formal leadership transition workshop with staff
- Engage in self-directed learning through books, tapes and/or seminars

Role: **Manager**

Primary focus:
Leading and Managing Programs

Core Competencies:
- Creativity & Innovation
- Financial Management
- Partnering
- Political Savvy
- Strategic Thinking
- Technology Management

Learning Experiences:
- Complete a 360˚ assessment and obtain/review results
- Be a mentor/have a mentor
- Participate in a detail outside of your current organization
- Within first year as new manager, conduct formal leadership transition workshop with staff
- Participate as a member of Governmental, Intergovernmental, and/or program task force committees
- Develop a learning contract/individual development plan based on 360˚ feedback
- Engage in self-directed learning through books, tapes and/or seminars
- Complete self-study online courses

Role: **Executive**

Primary focus:
Leading and Managing Organizations

Core Competencies:
- Entrepreneurship
- External Awareness
- Vision

Learning Experiences
- Complete a 360° assessment and obtain/review results
- Be a mentor/have a mentor
- Engage an executive coach
- Participate in executive-level task force committees
- Within first year as new executive, conduct formal leadership transition workshop with staff
- Complete self-study online courses
- Engage in self-directed learning through books, tapes and/or seminars

20

What is considered proficient for my role?

Proficiency is mastering the behavioral examples for your role. This guide contains behavioral examples for each of the leadership competencies for each of the roles.

A *behavioral example* is a success indicator showing how an employee at a particular level would demonstrate proficiency in a given competency. For example, a supervisor looking at behavioral example for conflict management would see "Actively involves employees and team or work unit in resolving differences over work issues (e.g., schedules, assignments, ensuring employee and organizational concerns are balanced)." An executive, on the other hand, might see "Provides resources and support to managers in resolving grievances and civil rights complaints that reach the executive level."

The behavioral examples can be used prior to beginning a learning experience to assess the need to develop that competency, during a longer learning experience to assess progress, and at the end of a learning experience to determine if further work is needed.

How Can I Use This Information?

First, you can use the behavioral examples to fully understand what a certain competency means for that specific leadership role. Having a clearer understanding will help you make a better development plan.

Second, you can also use the behavioral examples as an assessment of your current role. If the behavioral examples for your role show you to be proficient at that level and if you are interested in preparing for a position at the next leadership role, look at the behavioral examples at that next role as you begin to plan your development journey.

If all the competencies are important for all employees regardless of whether a person has an official leadership position, why are certain competencies linked to certain roles on the continuum?

When you look at the role continuum, the competencies listed at your role and below are the ones at which you should be proficient. The competencies listed at the role just above your level are the ones at which you should begin to develop proficiency. For competencies further up the role continuum, you should have an understanding of their functions and importance and be able to use them in a limited fashion.

Mastery of the leadership competencies provides you with a professional skill set that can be continually expanded and developed. Like the super left-footed soccer player, you might be better at a couple of the competencies than some of the others. I certainly hope so.

While each competency will not be needed all the time, once you have added a competency to your professional skill set, you can use it whenever you need it.

These competencies and the basic structure of them was developed over a number of years by staff at the U.S. Office of Personnel Management and are appropriate not just for the federal workforce, but for employees in nearly any organizational setting.

This framework shows the relationship of each competency to the goal of creating a workforce dedicated to producing results, serving customers, being honest and transparent, building successful teams and coalitions, being responsible stewards of resources, delivering on stakeholder needs, and creating good working environments for employees.

Chapter 2:
How to Develop Your Leadership Skills

Developing your leadership skills is fairly simple. Perhaps not easy, but simple, with just seven steps:

1. Identify your goal
2. Assess proficiency
3. Identify learning experiences
4. Create your development plan
5. Complete learning experiences
6. Assess progress
7. Repeat

You'll note that contrary to many improvement and developmental models, this model does not start with diagnosis first. This model begins with defining our leadership development goal, frequently in terms of a role or specific position. We do this to frame the developmental effort.

Many of us are eager to jump right to step number three, identify learning experiences. And why wouldn't we, as that's where things get fun? Don't. Start with your goal. As Stephen Covey preached, begin with the end in mind. And assessing your current state is also vitally necessary if you are going to truly increase your expertise. Showing alignment among your learning goals, your current proficiency level, and your proposed learning experiences will make a stronger case for leadership development requiring time and monetary commitments from your organization and support from your supervisor.

You can start your leadership development journey at any time. Sometimes it makes sense to have a set development cycle; for some organizations this development cycle begins at the start of the performance year. New employees or employees who change jobs during the performance year would work with their supervisors to begin their development within two months of starting the new job, and can lengthen or shorten the first development cycle to fit into the performance year. The development cycle may expand to cover one or two performance years, with the norm being one year. A two-year cycle might be desirable, for example, for an employee who is participating in a leadership course lasting more than 12 months. Don't wait for a set cycle; the time to improve yourself is now. Check with your supervisor to see what the leadership development cycle is within your organization.

How to develop your leadership skills
Step 1: Identify your goal

Review your position description, performance standards, and other guiding documents to become familiar with all of the requirements of your current job.

Think about where you would like to be one, two, five, or ten years down the road.

Review your organizational mission and values statements, structure, and strategic goals. Review these for not just the larger organization, but any teams that you are a part of. Think about how you would like to contribute to the mission and goals of your team, your program, your organization.

To identify the leadership competencies associated with your goals, locate your current role and the role on the continuum you are looking to land. Focus on developing proficiency in the competencies listed at your target role.

If your future goals include applying for a specific position, investigate that position. Identify the technical competencies you will need in order to demonstrate technical credibility in that position. You can identify needed technical competencies from a position description for that position. The position description may not list the specific leadership competencies needed for the position, but you may be able to figure those out by using the leadership role continuum.

The most powerful goals -- the ones that are most likely to get accomplished, and for us to realize that the goal was accomplished -- are SMART. They are Specific, Measurable, Attainable, Relevant, and Time-bound.

Specific goals are well defined and clear. We know what needs to be accomplished. We know what the "end in mind" looks like. We know the desired outcomes.

Measurable goals can be quantified. We know when we have accomplished the goal. We're not debating the definition of done. We have already decided in the goal.

Attainable goals can be reached. They are realistic given the constraints of resources, knowledge, and time. They may be a stretch. Perhaps you have heard the call from John F. Kennedy in a joint session to Congress on May 25th, 1961: "I believe that this nation should commit itself to achieving the goal, before this decade is out, of landing a man on the moon and returning him safely to the Earth." Was it a stretch? Yes. Was it attainable? Yes, indeed. Did we need to commit resources, brain power, and time? Of course, but any great goal is likely worth a little effort. Ensure your goals are attainable, even if they will require much in the way of resources, knowledge, and time.

Relevant goals are actually important and make an impact on achieving your larger objectives. Ask yourself if this goal really matters; relevant goals are burning bright with meaning for your greater objectives.

Time-bound goals have a determined end time. This isn't baseball, where there is no clock. This is lacrosse, where every second counts, because they're ticking down and when the horn goes off, that's the game. And, that's a time-bound goal. We know when it will be done by... or at least we know the target.

What might a decent SMART goal look like? Perhaps it might look something like this: "I will present at the employee lunch & learn at least once per quarter during the next fiscal year to both increase the pool of knowledge among my peers and to improve my confidence and presenting skills.

How to develop your leadership skills
Step 2: Assess Proficiency

Once you have determined the role you'd like to in, and the competencies you need to be successful in that role, you need to assess your current proficiency level. The gaps between your current performance and the competency level needed for a position will indicate which competencies you should first develop.

As you gather assessment information, first check that you are proficient in the competencies considered essential in your current leadership role and at roles below your current role. If assessments indicate you are proficient at those, focus on competencies for the next leadership role. Ask yourself, "Are you proficient at the competencies for your current role(s)?" If the answer is "no," work on the competencies for your current role(s). If the answer is "yes," work on the competencies for your next target role.

There are a variety of instruments you can use and actions you can take to assess your current competency levels.

Try using the behavioral examples for your current leadership role (and the next role if you are aspiring to move up the leadership role continuum) to self-assess your proficiency at each competency. Give copies to a colleague, your supervisor, or a customer and ask that person to rate you as well.

Discuss your level of performance with your supervisor and request suggestions on areas of development. Request the same type of information from peers, mentors, or others.

If you supervise others, use a 360° assessment to assess your proficiency at specific leadership competencies. I like the assessments published by FranklinCovey, the company a marriage of the minds of Hyrum Smith and Stephen Covey. You can find more information about the FranklinCovey assessments at https://assessments.franklincovey.com/.

If your work unit or program has administered a customer survey, use information from that survey if it refers to you or to your position or your work.

If available, take a preference assessment, like the Myers-Briggs Type Indicator (MBTI) or the DiSC Profile or the "What's My Communication Style" assessment. Results from preference assessments may provide further insight into the behavioral assessments described above. They serve as an input into our personal assessment of ourselves.

All of this, and more, serve as your inputs as you look to develop your leadership skills.

After assessing your proficiency, look back at the goals you set in Step 1. Refine or revise your goals based on the assessment information you have gathered. List the leadership competencies you wish to develop. These competencies to develop could be needs revealed by the assessments or strengths that you would like to further develop.

You can have more than one competency development goal in your development plan, but limit the number to three. Including too many competencies to develop dilutes your progress on any one of them. If you reach your goals on three competencies before the developmental cycle is finished, you can revise your development plan to add additional competencies. Remember, if you're in a situation where your supervisor is supporting your development plan, coordinate changes to the plan with your supervisor.

Also, I'm a fan of the strengths-based approach as popularized by Marcus Buckingham and Curt Coffman's *First, Break All the Rules*. From a strengths-based approach ask yourself, what are you good at? What are your strengths? Now, play to those. You're not looking for proficiency for those competencies. No, for these you are looking to maximize, to master the competency. If a particular leadership competency is a strength, if it comes naturally, perhaps, play to it; focus on it. Become phenomenal.

How to develop your leadership skills
Step 3: Identify Learning Experiences

A variety of ;learning activities and resources exist to assist you in accomplishing your learning goals.

Sometimes formal training is seen as the only method of learning. However, combining formal training, frequently seen as classroom training, with other activities (e.g., reading, community service, mentoring, and developmental detail assignments) is the most effective learning format.

Select the learning experiences that best match your learning style, the competency you are developing, and your program budget. Determine the dates by which you will complete the learning experiences you have identified.

Describe the evidence you will produce or actions you will take to demonstrate how you have increased proficiency in that competency. Part of this description should include how you will transfer what you have learned back to your job.

Many organizations require employees to list costs associated with the learning experience (e.g., tuition, travel, and course materials) and other resources needed to support your learning, (e.g., time away from work, technology, equipment, and access to particular people or information). Check with your supervisor for more information about how your organization support leadership development.

Some developmental programs also request that you demonstrate how your learning goals relate to and support your organization's mission and goals. If this link is required in your organization's leadership development program, review mission and vision statements, strategic goals, values statements, and workforce and succession planning documents. Then, describe how your proposed competency development goals and learning experiences will benefit the larger organization and your team.

If you work at an organization that doesn't support your leadership development, don't despair. There are many things you can do on your own, without organizational support, to work on your leadership competencies. We'll discuss them in the coming pages.

How to develop your leadership skills
Step 4: Create Your Development Plan

Whatever you call it, and whatever form it takes, you need a plan, a development plan, a leadership development plan. I've heard these called individual development plans or learning contracts.

It doesn't matter what you call it. You need a plan.

In an ideal world this plan would be in a document, not just ideas in your head. Ideally, the contents of this document are the result of conversation between you and your supervisor and would meet both personal and organizational needs. This written plan outlines your goals, lists your learning experiences, and records your progress.

The development plan should identify your learning goals. These goals should be related to competency. In addition, the plan lists resources and strategies for learning (e.g., classroom training, books, details, and developmental assignments) and identifies measurable outcomes to allow you and your Supervisor to assess your learning. The plan should specify completion dates for learning experiences and list the monetary costs for proposed learning experiences (e.g., travel, materials, books, tuition). A good development plan aligns the developmental goals with organizational and programmatic mission, values, strategic goals, and succession planning objectives.

Assemble the information you gathered in Steps 1 and 2 into a draft development plan. If you're in an organization that supports leadership development, give or send a copy to your supervisor and schedule a time to meet to review and complete the plan. During your meeting, discuss the entire development plan with your supervisor, explaining why you have selected those competencies and learning experiences. Be prepared to discuss how developing proficiency in those competencies will benefit you and your work unit and will increase your productivity.

A productive discussion with your supervisor should result in a mutually agreed-upon development plan and decisions regarding when and how you will meet to review progress, make necessary adjustments, and evaluate how well you have accomplished your learning goals.

If you are not in an organization that formally supports leadership development, you still need a plan. Your plan will not, in this case, be approved by your supervisor or anyone in the organization. The plan is for you. The learning elements will need to be things you can do on your own, without organizational support. Don't fret; sometimes the best leadership development plans are executed covertly, the benefits, however, being seen by everyone.

We will not always be a part of an organization that provides support. Once, when I transferred between federal agencies, I was two-thirds of the way through a formal leadership development program. My new supervisor was not supportive and told me that I could not use organizational time or resources to complete the program. I had to re-jigger my plan so that I could get the same learnings in an environment that didn't offer me support. Sometimes the learning comes in overcoming the challenges.

How to develop your leadership skills
Step 5: Complete Your Learning Experiences

This may sound like the easy part of the cycle. However, you may find that setting aside time in a busy schedule is difficult, particularly if you are doing an independent learning experience such as an online course or reading a book. If you set aside a short amount of time, as little as 15 minutes each day, to work on the learning experience, you will find that you can make faster progress than if you wait until you have a longer period of free time.

Many people find that scheduling 15 minutes first thing in the morning, before opening email, is best. Consider your learning preferences and select a time that works best for you. Remember, a little bit each day will help you progress faster than waiting for those larger chunks of free time that never seem to appear.

If your learning experience is a long-term learning experience, such as a detail, begin working on creating this experience as soon as you can. Don't procrastinate. For many formal leadership programs, you will be given a certain amount of time for the completion of the entire program. This will include the time-heavy experiences, such as details to another organization for a couple of months. Don't wait to try and set up something like this. Get started on finding the right experience. Too frequently, people find themselves scrambling for an appropriate learning experience in the allotted time frame.

How to develop your leadership skills
Step 6: Assess Progress

Schedule regular meetings with your supervisor to review progress on your competency development. Discuss how you have applied what you have learned to your job. If your learning goals change, meet with your supervisor to revise your development plan so it is up to date and accurately reflects your learning plans.

Your supervisor is a resource for developing your career plans and you can utilize his or her expertise throughout the development cycle.

At minimum, you should meet with your supervisor twice a year to discuss your goals, design a development plan, and review your accomplishments.

A leadership development discussion is not a performance appraisal review. Let that sink in.

This discussion about leadership development is an opportunity to clarify goals and to agree on actions and expected outcomes to improve in targeted competencies.

Here are some things you can do to help ensure you have a constructive and effective leadership development discussion with your supervisor:

- Dedicate specific, uninterrupted discussion time for the leadership development discussion.

- Initiate the discussion if needed. It does not matter whether you or your supervisor schedules the discussion. It matters that it happens!

- Go over the entire development plan with your supervisor. Be prepared for possible changes to your plans. For example, your supervisor might disagree with your own assessment on some competencies, might know of better resources for developing a certain competency, or might not have enough in the budget for one of your proposed learning activities.

- Finalize a mutually agreed-upon development plan during the meeting. You can enter the agreed-upon changes into the plan after the meeting, but you should come to agreement on the contents of the plan while you are together.

- Establish dates for "check in" follow- up meetings to revisit your development plan, report progress, and adjust timelines, goals, and measurements, as necessary.

Developing leadership competencies is a joint effort of every employee and that employee's supervisor.

As an employee, discuss your career goals with your supervisor and work with them to assess the leadership competencies you will need to reach those goals. If your supervisor does not approach you for a discussion, you need to initiate that discussion.

As a supervisor, set aside time for employee developmental meetings during which you help your employees refine their career goals, assess their proficiency at the needed competencies, create development plans, and assess their progress.

Both parties to this development plan have specific roles in planning for successful growth and development.

What if your supervisor does not support your development or, for some reason, you can't rely on your supervisor? Is this case, you may find it helpful to find someone, a mentor or an accountability partner, who can provide the supervisory input, counsel, and support.

Take ownership of your own leadership development.

You, as the employee or learner, should:

- Identify your learning goals.

- Identify resources and strategies for meeting your learning objectives and the costs involved.

- Identify how you will demonstrate that you have accomplished your learning objectives and how you will use what you have learned.

- Demonstrate how your learning objectives link to your program's vision, mission, and strategic goals.

- Meet with your supervisor to discuss your plan and finalize your development plan.

- Review progress with your supervisor every six months.
- Complete all learning experiences.

- Assess your progress and begin the development cycle again.

You, as the Supervisor, should:

- Assist in creating a development plan.

- Guide the learner toward useful resources for development.

- Review the development plan and provide feedback.
- Ensure the employee's goals are aligned with the program mission, vision, and current needs.

- Schedule regular meetings (at minimum, twice per year) to discuss progress, application, and further development.

- Make adjustments, if necessary, to ensure development plans of all employees can be accomplished within the training budget.

- Support transfer of learning by providing employees opportunities to practice new skills and by rewarding improved performance.

When you develop others,
you touch the future.

Transferring Learning to the Job

Learning goes beyond what you pick up in a classroom or other learning situations. The best way to reinforce learning, increase your competence, and improve your performance is to practice and use what you have learned on the job.

One way to successfully transfer learning back to the job is to consciously identify ways to use what you have learned and to get feedback and coaching from peers, mentors, or others who can observe you using your new knowledge and skills.

Mentoring and Coaching

A mentor is a role model and sounding board who provides confidential guidance. A mentor is someone, not in the employee's chain of command, who is in a position to help with job and career goals, and who is committed to doing so. Mentoring is a constantly evolving process and requires the mentor and protégé work together as partners to define appropriate mentoring goals and to provide each other with sufficient feedback to enable the achievement of those goals.

A coach assists in review and self-reflection and helps recipients apply book or classroom knowledge to their current work situation. This reflection helps those receiving the coaching learn how to analyze and resolve the leadership challenges they are facing. Supervisors, Managers, and Executives often find a coach especially valuable when facing the challenges of a new leadership position.

How to develop your leadership skills
Step 7: Repeat

Life goes on. If you're not getting smarter, you're not keeping up with your peers. Continuous learning, continuous improvement is necessary to succeed in these turbulent times. Take a breath, and return to Step 1.

Life is a journey.

Life is a cycle.

Life is a process.

Life is what you make it.

Make it count:

Get back up and do it again.

Chapter 3:
Leadership Development for All Employees

Primary focus:
Managing and Leading Yourself

Core Competencies:
- Continual Learning
- Cross-Cultural Interactions
- Customer Service
- Flexibility
- Integrity/Honesty
- Interpersonal Skills
- Oral Communication
- Problem Solving
- Resilience
- Written Communication

Leadership Role Continuum
All Employees --> Team Leader --> Supervisor --> Manager --> Executive

---

Leadership is a Role for All Employees

Some employees think they do not need to develop leadership skills because they are not Supervisors or Managers. In reality, every employee is a leader. Employees lead through their actions and words, by example, and by influencing others. All employees need to develop a strong foundation of leadership skills to perform better in their current and future positions

Whether or not we are designated as leaders because of our position, it is the responsibility of each individual member of the organization to take ownership of developing their own leadership competencies.

For the role of All Employees, ten leadership competencies are essential. While all the competencies are important, some are more important than others for some roles. If I were an individual contributor and was looking at improving myself within this role, I would start by looking at the essential competencies. On the competency sheets (following shortly) these competencies are identified as "focused for all employees." The remaining competencies are not to be neglected, but for the all employee role, they are less important. On the competency sheets, these are identified as "appropriate for all employees."

Behavioral Examples and the Leadership Competencies

The Behavioral Examples illustrate how each competency is used within each leadership role. For example, with the All-Employee role, behavioral examples for "Developing Others" (at the supervisor level on the continuum) illustrate that you would use this competency on a more individual basis than a supervisor would. You could help train a new employee or share newly gained knowledge with your colleagues. Behavioral examples for someone in the supervisor role, on the other hand, illustrate responsibility for ensuring development resources are fairly distributed among all employees.

If you haven't yet read Chapter 2, now would be a good time to go back and read it.

Perhaps you are wondering how your supervisor is involved in your development plan. Great question. If you are in an organization that supports individual development plans, your supervisor likely needs to approve your development plan. If you are in an organization that does not institutionally support development plans, you can still benefit from sharing your development plan with you supervisor. Your supervisor could be instrumental in identifying resources, providing support, and assisting with your assessment.

You can use this guide to create your development plan on your own, only scheduling a meeting to discuss your plans once you have developed them. Or, you can seek your supervisor's assistance and input at any stage in the developmental process.

Leadership Development for All Employees
Step 1: Identify Your Goals

To begin identifying your goals, ask yourself the following questions:

- What are my developmental goals?
- Where do I want to be in one year or three to five years?
- Do I want to be proficient in my current position?
- Do I want to laterally move to another position?
- Do I want to move to a Project Manager or Team Leader position, or even higher to a Supervisor, Manager, or Executive position?
- Do I have a specific leadership level in mind or even a specific position in mind?
- What sorts of social, technological, governmental changes might be headed our way that will impact my future, and, thus, my goals?

Once you have identified your goals, think about the competencies that would be necessary for those goals and possible roles. What competencies will you need to grow as you move forward? What do you know you're strong in that will help carry the water for that role? Generate a list of competencies associated with both attaining your goal and maintaining that goal.

Now, build your goals. Goals ought to be SMART (Specific, Measureable, Attainable, Realistic, and Time-bound). See Chapter 2 for more about SMART goals.

Leadership Development for All Employees
Step 2: Assess Proficiency

Once you have identified the competencies, it is essential to assess your proficiency in those competencies. First, assess the competencies essential to your leadership role. At the "All-Employee" role, these include:

- Continual Learning
- Customer Service
- Flexibility
- Interpersonal Skills
- Integrity/Honesty
- Oral Communication
- Problem Solving
- Public Service Motivation
- Resilience
- Written Communication

To assess proficiency in these competencies, use the behavioral examples provided in the next few pages. As you read these behavioral examples and decide whether you are able to successfully perform the tasks associated with each example.

If your assessments show mastery of the competencies above, repeat the assessment process using the behavioral examples for the non-targeted behavioral examples. When you finish assessing, select two or three competencies on which to focus and move to the next step. Don't pick more than three competencies to work on, and even three is frequently too many. You can't make changes without focus; with too many things to work on, you can't focus. The other thing to remember is that you are in for the long haul; you don't need to make improvements in every aspect of your life right now. You have time; take advantage of that. Pick one or two things to work on now. Master those, and you can work on the next competency or two.

Leadership Development for All Employees
Step 3: Identify Learning Experiences

Once you have assessed your proficiency, the next step is to select learning experiences to either address any proficiency gaps you identified during your assessment or to move you to a higher master level for any strengths you identified during your assessment. Don't only focus on your opportunities for improvement when looking for developmental opportunities. Feel free to feed your strengths.

To be considered development, the learning experiences you list in your development plan should result in changes on the job. That is to say, we should see you incorporating new knowledge, new skills, and new tools in your work. Those who work with you should be able to see you taking on a new task or handling a stressful situation easier or making tighter presentations.

For true learning to occur,
pair knowledge-gaining experiences
with practicing experiences.

To apply your learning on the job requires that you combine practice with knowledge acquisition. Take a course or read a book or listen to a podcast or watch a video, and you have what was once referred to as "book knowledge." This passive knowledge needs to be turned in to action for any development of the individual to take place. You must pair the learning with some doing. Take a course on active listening; practice what you learned. Try to pair action with all your learning activities.

Leadership Development for All Employees
Step 4: Create Your Development Plan

Next, create a development plan. Development plans can take a variety of formats. Some organizations have formal development plans which are part of a cloud-based human resources offering. Other organizations use spreadsheets. I like a good sheet of paper. Not matter the format, that content is similar. Most development plans gather details about the goal, the description of the goal, the learning activities to be completed, and costs.

For a real example of a development plan, see https://drive.google.com/file/d/0BwOicNLrhtBnMjc2NjMzZjltY2U 1NC00NmQ3LTk4MjEtY2JhOGU2ZGRlZmQ1/view?usp=sharing. Yes, that's mine from a past role. If that URL is too much, try this QR code:

Leadership Development for All Employees
Step 5: Complete Learning Experiences

Once you have an approved development plan, it's time to get working.

Who should approve your development plan? If you're flying solo, you have no hoops to jump through. For those operating in an organization that supports development plans, check with your supervisor. In most organizations, the supervisor approves plans for their own subordinates.

Begin working on the learning experiences identified in your plan. Keep a journal of your activities and reflections and learnings. Without self awareness and self reflection, the learning will less likely take root. Record the completion date for each learning experience.

Leadership Development for All Employees
Step 6: Assess Progress

After you have completed your learning experiences, and have solidified those learnings with action, reassess your proficiency in the competencies associated with this role.

Use the behavioral examples to self-assess.

Leadership Development for All Employees
Step 7: Repeat.

What can we say? It's a cycle: rinse and repeat.

Leadership Development for All Employees
Behavioral Examples

The following behavioral examples describe typical actions for the All-Employee role. The focus here is on managing yourself.

The behavioral examples are divided into two groups of competencies. The first group are the competencies which target the all-employee role. There are ten competencies which target all employees. The second group of competencies are all the rest. All employees do have behavioral examples of these competences, but these competencies do not target the all-employee role.

In both groups, the competencies are listed in alphabetical order. All of these behavioral examples describe actions that would be used at the All-Employee level.

Use the behavioral examples to assess your proficiency. If you think you need to work on a more than three competencies, take a deep breath and re-evaluate. Focus on two, three tops, first. You can come back for me; I hope you do. Start first on focus competencies you want to tackle, then move on to the rest.

Behavioral Examples Targeted for All Employees

Competency: Continual Learning

Definition: Assesses and recognizes own strengths and weaknesses. Pursues self-development.

Behavioral Examples for the All Employee Role

- Actively seeks feedback on own performance.

- Actively seeks learning in areas beyond own technical expertise in order to become a productive employee.

- Assesses own strengths and weaknesses.

- Crafts and uses a variety of learning approaches, including formal coursework, reading, talking with others, attending formal training, shadowing, detail assignments, and on-the-job experiences for own development.

- Seeks challenging assignments and unfamiliar tasks.

- Seeks out and engages in opportunities for self-improvement.

- Spends time learning from others.

- Uses a development plan to link assessments, career goals, and organizational strategies to personal development plans.

Behavioral Examples Targeted for All Employees

Competency: **Cross-Cultural Interactions**

Definition: Interacts with people of other cultures with ease. Communicates and performs over distance, culture, and time differences. Understands the impact of culture on management strategy and style.

Behavioral Examples for the All Employee Role

- Reads books about diverse cultures in order to understand them better.

- Reaches out to new, nontraditional groups to educate them about the work of the organization.

- Is open to the contributions of diverse colleagues, employees, and stakeholders; seeks and acknowledges their input.

- Creates an informal cross-cultural advisor team to help share knowledge about different cultures within the group to increase the pool of knowledge about these cultures.

- Understands values, behaviours and perceptions that stem from differing cultural backgrounds and finds natural commonalities to bridge those differences.

Behavioral Examples Targeted for All Employees

Competency: **Customer Service**

Definition: Anticipates and meets the needs of both internal and external customers. Delivers high-quality products and services. Demonstrates commitment to continuous improvement.

Behavioral Examples for the All Employee Role

- Demonstrates empathy for customers.

- Follows through on customers' questions, requests, and complaints.

- Gains customer confidence through competence, good communications, and trust.

- Gives clear explanations; uses plain language to clarify needs and interests with customers.

- Responds efficiently to requests for help, information, and services.

- Recognizes coworkers as customers and responds to them accordingly.

- Takes personal responsibility for dealing with and/or correcting customer service issues and concerns.

- Treats all with respect and consideration.

Behavioral Examples Targeted for All Employees

Competency: **Flexibility**

Definition: Demonstrates an openness to change and new information; rapidly adapts to new information, changing conditions, or unexpected obstacles.

Behavioral Examples for the All Employee Role

- Adapts behavior and work methods, as needed, in response to new information, changing conditions, or unexpected obstacles.

- Adopts a positive attitude to new demands and is optimistic and accepting of necessary change.

- Modifies communications techniques, as necessary, in order to reach understanding with and among different groups.

- Demonstrates a willingness to learn and use new procedures and technology.

- Responds appropriately to the differing needs of diverse internal and external customer groups.

- Sees the possibilities in the situation.

- Smoothly handles multiple demands, shifting priorities, and rapid change.

- Understands one's own preferences and habits of thought and demonstrates the ability to "flex" from preferred styles into those most appropriate to the circumstance.

Behavioral Examples Targeted for All Employees

Competency: **Integrity and Honesty**

Definition: Behaves in an honest, fair, and ethical manner. Shows consistency in words and actions. Creates a culture that fosters high ethical standards.

Behavioral Examples for the All Employee Role

- Accepts personal responsibility and does not shift the blame to others.

- Acts out of motivation to do the right thing, rather than out of pleasure, fear, inclination, habit, peer approval, or social or political pressure.

- Does not make promises that are expedient but cannot be kept.

- Expresses dissent when actions or pending decisions would violate organizational values, laws, and regulations.

- Holds self accountable for meeting objectives and keeping commitments; follows through.

- Demonstrates the ability to be fair and ethical with customers and employees.

- Keeps organizational and personal information confidential when required and/or appropriate.

- Refrains from spreading gossip, rumor, and false information; honors the absent.

Behavioral Examples Targeted for All Employees

Competency: **Interpersonal Skills**

Definition: Treats others with courtesy, sensitivity, and respect. Considers and appropriately responds to the needs and feelings of different people in different situations.

Behavioral Examples for the All Employee Role

- Builds consensus through give and take.

- Builds trust through one's reliability and authenticity.

- Considers and appropriately responds to the needs, feelings, and capabilities of different people in different situations.

- Seeks to understand the culture, beliefs, values, biases, preferences, feelings, and other drivers of behavior -- both conscious and unconscious -- in oneself and others.

- Demonstrates discretion and tact when correcting or questioning another's idea or action.

- Seeks accurate information, avoids jumping to conclusions, or passing on questionable information.

- Seeks feedback from others to avoid blind spots that can cause misunderstandings.

- Demonstrates respect for the values and ideas of others, even while not agreeing with them.

- Demonstrates understanding, tact, and concern for others.

Behavioral Examples Targeted for All Employees

Competency: **Oral Communication**

Definition: Makes clear and convincing oral presentations to individuals and groups. Listens effectively. Clarifies information as needed. Facilitates open communication

Behavioral Examples for the All Employee Role

- Actively checks to ensure the message has been understood.

- Looks for visual feedback from others and uses questions to check understanding.

- Considers the audience members, their familiarity with the topic, and degree of interest prior to speaking.

- Demonstrates articulate, clear, concise, and effective in communicating with others.

- Demonstrates the ability to be prepared to listen to other views, flexible, and to modify own perspectives.

- Recognizes and utilizes a variety of communication preferences (e.g., public or private, visual or auditory).

- Speaks in a way that makes complex technical concepts understandable and uses appropriate supporting materials (charts, illustrations, etc.).

- Uses common conventions of language and grammar appropriate to professional settings.

- Appropriately uses gesture, eye contact, vocal pitch and intensity to positively add to the impact of the message.

Behavioral Examples Targeted for All Employees

Competency: **Problem Solving**

Definition: Identifies and analyzes problems. Weighs relevance and accuracy of information. Generates and evaluates alternative solutions. Makes recommendations.

Behavioral Examples for the All Employee Role

- Demonstrates the ability to predict objections and takes these into account.

- Continually seeks better ways to accomplish work through alternatives.

- Demonstrates the ability to think critically. Uses knowledge of assumptions, mental models, systems archetypes, as well as the context -- such as political trends, priorities, and cultures -- to anticipate problems and to recognize a need for change.

- Evaluates complex situations and ideas; clearly identifies and frames the problem; sorts out symptoms from root causes.

- Challenges and provides alternatives to generally accepted practice.

- Evaluates and adjusts solutions when they do not meet customers' needs or fit the situation.

- Identifies issues, within the context of own job, that require decisions or other action.

- Works to fix the problem, not to blame.

Behavioral Examples Targeted for All Employees

Competency: **Resilience**

Definition: Deals effectively with pressure. Remains optimistic and persistent, even under adversity. Quickly recovers from setbacks.

Behavioral Examples for the All Employee Role

- Balances priorities at work with personal life concerns and wellness.

- Continues to move projects forward despite setbacks, e.g., by trying different approaches to reach a goal.

- During change, assists team/work group members to handle uncertainty and to persevere.

- Calmly handles crises and stressful situations.

- Handles personal assumptions and "gut" reactions of fear, anger, and sadness.

- Demonstrates self-awareness and understands situations that are personal stress triggers and how stress affects performance.

- Tolerates change and flux.

- Seeks support from friends, professionals, or peers during crisis periods.

Behavioral Examples Targeted for All Employees

Competency: **Written Communication**

Definition: Writes in a clear, concise, organized, and convincing manner for the intended audience.

Behavioral Examples for the All Employee Role

- Accurately fills in or completes forms, logs, files, and such.

- Adheres to organizational policy for all written communications, guidelines, and electronic communication and documents.

- Brings to the attention of the Manager when customers or stakeholders may benefit from written information.

- Conveys information highlighting essential points and clearly conveys the message of the subject to the intended audience at the level of the receiver.

- Creates an informative subject line and is clear and concise in e-mail messages.

- Ensures written text is carefully edited for perspective, accuracy, and correctness.

- Issues information via the appropriate medium (e.g., e-mail, written memos).

- Makes written work clear, easy to follow, concise, and relevant.

- Uses a written style and vocabulary appropriate to the audience.

Behavioral Examples for All Employees

Competency: **Accountability**

Definition: Holds self and others accountable for measurable high-quality, timely, and cost-effective results. Determines objectives, sets priorities, and delegates work. Accepts responsibility for mistakes. Complies with established control systems and rules.

Behavioral Examples for the All Employee Role

- Demonstrates strong ethics and professionalism.

- Holds self accountable for own mistakes.

- Holds self accountable for achieving results within assigned deadlines.

- Protects employee, customer, and stakeholder privacy.

- Ensures projects are completed on time, within budget, and to the customer's satisfaction.

- Understands own role as a public servant and the responsibilities of government to the people.

- Uses internal controls and monitoring systems to protect the integrity of the organization and prevent waste, fraud, and mismanagement, reporting any instances where such problems occur.

Behavioral Examples for All Employees

Competency: **Conflict Management**

Definition: Encourages creative tension and differences of opinions. Anticipates and takes steps to prevent counterproductive confrontations. Manages and resolves conflicts and disagreements in a constructive manner.

Behavioral Examples for the All Employee Role

- Assists in clarifying issues that have caused conflict or concern.

- Can express one's position and feelings clearly and concisely without accusation, sarcasm, or hostility.

- Handles difficult people with diplomacy.

- Demonstrates discretion and tact when correcting or questioning another's idea or action.

- Manages own emotions.

- Seeks points of agreement between own views and those of others.

- Uses good communication to proactively discuss differences with coworkers, Supervisors, and the public in an effort to create a positive atmosphere.

- Uses interest-based approaches to resolve conflict with colleagues and customers

Behavioral Examples for All Employees

Competency: **Creativity and Innovation**

Definition: Develops new insights into situations. Questions conventional approaches. Encourages new ideas and innovations. Designs and implements new or cutting-edge products and services.

Behavioral Examples for the All Employee Role

- Continually seeks better ways to accomplish work.

- Demonstrates openness to new or unconventional ideas and solutions.

- Finds ways to initiate improvements within one's sphere of influence.

- Habitually explores multiple, sometimes unconventional, options and different perspectives in order to gain the best solution.

- Suggests ways to improve quality and efficiency.

- Supports and encourages colleagues with new ideas.

- Uses full range of skills, knowledge, and experiences to imagine and actively promote improvements.

Behavioral Examples for All Employees

Competency: **Decisiveness**

Definition: Makes effective and timely decisions, even when data are limited or solutions produce unpleasant consequences. Perceives the impact and implications of decisions.

Behavioral Examples for the All Employee Role

- Demonstrates the ability to distinguish between personal preferences and objectively preferable courses of action.

- Commits to action to carry out assignments; acts promptly and effectively once a decision on a course of action has been made.

- Makes appropriate, informed decisions on technical matters or work processes.

- Makes sound and timely decisions for activities within own area of responsibility, consulting others as appropriate.

- Refers decisions upward only when necessary and appropriate.

- Takes responsibility for own decisions.

- Persists with decisions unless reliable and credible information indicates a better course of action.

- Sees and seizes opportunities to make things happen to make a positive difference.

Behavioral Examples for All Employees

Competency: **Developing Others**

Definition: Develops the ability of others to perform and contribute to the organization by providing ongoing feedback and by providing opportunities to learn through formal and informal methods.

Behavioral Examples for the All Employee Role

- Assists new employees in understanding the organizational (and team) mission and goals.

- Assists with training of new and/or current employees in areas of own expertise.

- Collaborates and shares plans, information, and resources.

- Is sought out by peers for expertise and counsel.

- Attentively listens to others to hear and understand what is being said, and to assess what is meant.

- Passes on information about training opportunities to coworkers.

- Shares information learned in training opportunities (in formal courses, details, and reading) with coworkers.

- Influences and inspires others to develop their skills.

Behavioral Examples for All Employees

Competency: **Entrepreneurship**

Definition: Positions the organization for future success by identifying new opportunities. Builds the organization by developing or improving products or services. Takes calculated risks to accomplish organizational objectives.

Behavioral Examples for the All Employee Role

- Demonstrates an ability to create new services and products.

- Asks "what if" questions to test assumptions and challenge the *status quo*.

- Assesses potential risks while suggesting and developing modifications to products or service delivery.

- Makes innovative suggestions and tries new approaches within own area of work.

- Participates in projects improving work unit processes, procedures, environment, and customer service.

- Seeks better solutions instead of falling back on quick answers, looks beyond the obvious.

Behavioral Examples for All Employees

Competency: **External Awareness**

Definition: Understands and keeps up to date on local, national, and international policies and trends that affect the organization and shape stakeholders' views. Demonstrates awareness of the organization's impact on the external environment.

Behavioral Examples for the All Employee Role

- Demonstrates knowledge of how one's own activities fit into the bigger picture, both as regards the policy issues as well as organizational structure and processes.

- Demonstrates the ability to define one's self in the context of relationship with others.

- Demonstrates an awareness of related work done through other disciplines and of other groups within the organization.

- Keeps up to date with relevant laws, regulations, policies, and procedures affecting the organization.

- Knows about other organization services and/or information that might be relevant to the customer.

- Seeks broad understanding of those who affect and who are affected by one's work.

- Stays knowledgeable of developing policy and policy issues in one's field.

- Supports the need for changes in direction and priorities due to external change

Behavioral Examples for All Employees

Competency: **Financial Management**

Definition: Understands the organization's financial processes. Prepares, justifies, and administers the program budget. Supports procurement and contracting to achieve desired results. Monitors expenditures and uses cost-benefit thinking to set priorities.

Behavioral Examples for the All Employee Role

- Completes projects within budget projections.

- Demonstrates an ability to be ethical and frugal in using organizational resources.

- Provides budget figures for projects in own area of work.

- Suggests improvements that conserve labor hours, reduce supply/equipment/facility costs, and improve quality.

- Tracks and controls expenditures for assigned projects and budgets.

- Understands the constraints and accountability inherent in acquisition and contracting tools, procedures, processes, and systems. Solicits quotes from vendors.

- Uses comparative data when selecting contractors or vendors.

- Effectively and efficiently uses materials and supplies to minimize expenses

Behavioral Examples for All Employees

Competency: **Human Capital Management**

Definition: Builds and manages workforce based on organizational goals, budget considerations, and staffing needs. Ensures employees are appropriately recruited, selected, appraised, and rewarded. Takes action to address performance problems. Manages a multi-sector workforce and a variety of work situations.Here

Behavioral Examples for the All Employee Role

- Understands systems and programs assisting employees against discriminatory practice.

- Understands procedures and official assistance for reporting unlawful, abusive, or endangering behaviors.

- Keeps supervisors apprised of workload, especially of major changes in workload.

- Maintains communication with supervisor on developmental needs.

- Suggests appropriate recognition methods for coworkers.

- Understands immunity from reprisal for reporting unlawful behavior, mismanagement, gross waste of funds, abuse of authority, or substantial and specific danger to public health or safety

Behavioral Examples for All Employees

Competency: **Influencing and Negotiating**

Definition: Persuades others. Builds consensus through give and take. Gains cooperation from others to obtain information and accomplish goals.

Behavioral Examples for the All Employee Role

- Builds positive relationships throughout the immediate workgroup and with key members of other workgroups.

- Effectively argues and defends a point of view to influence the outcome.

- Clarifies others' understanding of the issue or situation.

- Effectively employs negotiation techniques, such as interest-based bargaining, to facilitate "win-win" outcomes and agreements.

- Expresses empathy and earns the trust of others.

- Routinely questions one's own possible role in the creation of misunderstanding or dissent.

- Recognizes how the issues at hand affect other people, and demonstrates awareness of the consequences.

Behavioral Examples for All Employees

Competency: **Leveraging Diversity**

Definition: Fosters an inclusive workplace where diversity and individual differences are valued and leveraged to achieve the vision and mission of the organization.

Behavioral Examples for the All Employee Role

- Actively pursues knowledge and understanding of perspectives and ideas not one's own.
- Demonstrates belief in the concept of human dignity; treating all others with consideration, respect, and fairness, and openly, consistently challenging bias, intolerance, and incivility.
- Demonstrates support for diversity strategies that strengthen service delivery, e.g., through use of bilingual and alternate formats (large type or Braille) for forms, letters, signs, and pamphlets, for a diverse customer base.
- Employs a basic knowledge of individual and cultural differences to understand that the same message may be understood quite differently depending on the context.
- Demonstrates sensitivity to cross-cultural issues, cultural differences, nonverbal cues, feelings, and emotions.
- Supports a workplace culture that welcomes and values new thought, different perspectives, and nonconventional approaches.
- Supports the valuable role diversity can play in keeping thinking flexible and appropriate to changing circumstances.
- Effectively works with customers, peers, and stakeholders from all backgrounds.

Behavioral Examples for All Employees

Competency: **Partnering**

Definition: Develops networks and builds alliances. Collaborates across boundaries to build strategic relationships and achieve common goals.

Behavioral Examples for the All Employee Role

- Broadens own understanding of how fields of knowledge, programs, and service skills overlap.

- Builds customer and employee networks and contacts to support work in own area.

- Develops professional relationships with colleagues inside and outside the organization.

- Develops contacts to gain broader understanding and context for own work.

- Finds common ground with industry representatives, stakeholders, customers, and employees to ensure effective working relationships.

- Liaises within own department to solve problems.

- Positively responds and reciprocates when approached by others.

Behavioral Examples for All Employees

Competency: **Political Savvy**

Definition: Identifies the internal and external politics impacting the work of the organization. Perceives organizational and political reality and acts accordingly.

Behavioral Examples for the All Employee Role

- Demonstrates the ability to identify opponents and why they take a certain position on an issue.

- Demonstrates the ability to identify who is affected, who loses and who gains from a particular action, and other potential consequences.

- Successfully works within a wide range of environments and contexts (physical, virtual, small and large groups, organizational methods, processes, and cultures).

- Demonstrates knowledge of how one's own activities fit into the bigger picture including with regard to policies, organizational structure, and processes.

- Recognizes when to compromise and when to remain firm to accomplish broader organizational objectives affecting projects.

- Demonstrates the ability to identify the relationships within the environment and with coworkers, supervisors, customers, contractors, and policy makers.

- Demonstrates the ability to identify who the key stakeholders in one's own work area are and keep them informed of important situations.

- Understands political forces within an organization.

Behavioral Examples for All Employees

Competency: **Strategic Thinking**

Definition: Formulates objectives and priorities and implements plans consistent with the long-term interests of the organization in a global environment. Capitalizes on opportunities and manages risks.Here

Behavioral Examples for the All Employee Role

- Demonstrates a broad knowledge of own field and seeks knowledge in other areas that influence or are related to it.

- Adroitly shifts direction and redirects efforts when changes are implemented.

- Forms contingency plans to overcome potential obstacles, and to take advantage of unforeseeable opportunities.

- Provides ideas and information to Supervisor and team/work unit members on possible enhancements or impediments to organizational performance.

- Thinks strategically and suggests processes or procedures within the unit to avert problems and accomplish goals.

- Demonstrates the ability to explain how work unit activities and priorities relate to strategic goals.

- Identifies the basic issues, context, and customer concerns as addressed in the Agency's mission.

- Demonstrates the ability to link one's daily work to goals and strategies of the organization.

Behavioral Examples for All Employees

Competency: **Team Building**

Definition: Inspires and fosters team commitment, spirit, pride, and trust. Facilitates cooperation and motivates team members to accomplish group goals.

Behavioral Examples for the All Employee Role

- Actively contributes to the development of team/work group goals and works toward the accomplishment of those goals.

- Demonstrates the ability to be effective in drawing out the opinions and ideas of group members.

- Demonstrates a proactive approach to defusing arguments among peers.

- Optimistically deals with negativity in presence of other employees, such as by refusing to pass on gossip and recognizing positive contributions of colleagues by vocalizing recognition.

- Recognizes and values the talents of others.

- Supports team decisions, and is a good team player. Demonstrates honesty and responsibility and performs fair share of the work.

- Works with colleagues in a collaborative, inclusive, outcome-oriented manner.

Behavioral Examples for All Employees

Competency: **Technical Credibility**

Definition: Understands and appropriately applies principles, procedures, requirements, regulations, and policies related to specialized expertise.

Behavioral Examples for the All Employee Role

- Performs accurate work in a timely and efficient manner.

- Keeps knowledge current and seeks opportunities to broaden and enhance cross-functional expertise.

- Applies new skills, techniques, and procedures in own area of work.

- Consults with technical experts as needed.

- Seeks information on procedures, regulations, and policies that will affect work.

- Shares information related to area of expertise with coworkers

Behavioral Examples for All Employees

Competency: **Technology Management**

Definition: Keeps up to date on technological developments. Makes effective use of technology to achieve results. Ensures access to and security of technology systems.

Behavioral Examples for the All Employee Role

- Employs IT to improve performance, communicate better, achieve the organization's goals, and to fulfill its mission.

- Follows established computer security procedures to protect integrity/confidentiality of records.

- Demonstrates proficiency in using technology applications used to support one's work and communications.

- Keeps technology skills up to date through practice as well as other continual learning approaches.

- Suggests areas where technological improvements might be implemented in serving the customer.

- Effectively uses technology to ensure work tasks are performed more efficiently

Behavioral Examples for All Employees

Competency: **Vision**

Definition: Takes a long-term view and builds a shared vision with others. Acts as a catalyst for organizational change. Influences others to translate vision into action.

Behavioral Examples for the All Employee Role

- Demonstrates the ability to explain how one's work contributes to the organization's and team's vision and mission. Demonstrates allegiance to mission.

- Consistently thinks about whether an approach process or service can be improved.

- Creates personal development plans and goals linked to serving the organization's mission.

- Makes a conscious effort to broaden own perspective and thinking.

- Provides support to fellow employees in accomplishing the mission.

- Refers to the big picture and tries to understand others' perspectives

Chapter 4:
Leadership Development for Team Leaders

Primary focus:
Leading Teams and Managing Projects

Core Competencies:
- Decisiveness
- Influencing/Negotiating
- Technical Credibility
- Team Building

Leadership Role Continuum
All Employees --> **Team Leader** --> Supervisor --> Manager --> Executive

---

Are you in a team leader role or want to be in a team leader role? Here are the leadership competencies and the behavioral examples for the role of team leader.

Follow the process as outlined in Chapter 2:

1. Identify your goal
2. Assess proficiency
3. Identify learning experiences
4. Create your development plan
5. Complete learning experiences
6. Assess progress
7. Repeat

As you work though your development plan, review the behavioral examples on the following pages. These examples should provide you with a fairly comprehensive view of what the leadership competencies look like for the role of team leader.

Behavioral Examples Targeted for Team Leaders

Competency: **Decisiveness**

Definition: Makes effective and timely decisions, even when data is limited or solutions produce unpleasant consequences. Perceives the impact and implications of decisions.

Behavioral Examples for the Team Leader Role

- Advises team members and stakeholders of possible impact of decisions and actions.

- Builds knowledge from past experiences into decision-making process. Consults others when changes in regulations, customer needs, or circumstances necessitate a major change in the team project.

- Ensures team decisions are aligned with and support the organization's mission, vision, and goals.

- Evaluates the impact of decisions.

- Demonstrates knowledge of ethical decision-making tools as well as Federal ethics regulations and other laws that might pertain to a particular situation.

- Makes good decisions even where there are competing and ambiguous priorities.

- Seeks legal and ethical advice when questions arise, or actions to be taken are unclear.

- Understands operational implications of strategy and can look beyond solutions that are merely expedient.

Behavioral Examples Targeted for Team Leaders

Competency: **Influencing and Negotiating**

Definition: Persuades others. Builds consensus through give and take. Gains cooperation from others to obtain information and accomplish goals.

Behavioral Examples for the Team Leader Role

- Builds consensus on team project goals and processes to reach those goals.

- Effectively employs a variety of negotiation techniques allowing different parties to reach mutually agreeable solutions.

- Facilitates the working relationship between the organization and the team.

- Identifies and understands the interests and positions of others in the negotiation process.

- Demonstrates the ability to be alert to means and opportunities to inform the larger organization and other stakeholders of the credibility and value of the group's work, to solicit support, and gain buy-in.

- Demonstrates skill at reframing an issue so alternate perspectives and opposite views can be understood, and perhaps, accommodated.

- Networks to form new relationships and strengthen currently existing ones.

- Effectively represents the group throughout the organization.

Behavioral Examples Targeted for Team Leaders

Competency: **Team Building**

Definition: Inspires and fosters team commitment, spirit, pride, and trust. Facilitates cooperation and motivates team members to accomplish group goals.

Behavioral Examples for the Team Leader Role

- Coaches, mentors, and guides teams and team members in such a way as to foster commitment, team spirit, pride, and trust.

- Empowers team members to resolve issues and make changes that benefit customers.

- Encourages and models inclusiveness.

- Facilitates group process to help team members effectively work to solve problems, make group decisions, and accomplish goals.

- Fosters team identity through meaningful formal or informal recognition.

- Helps clarify team purpose, goals, roles, and responsibilities.

- Involves all team members and ensures all voices are heard and respected.

- Recommends awards and recognition to recognize individual and team performance when work supports organizational goals and achieves results.

Behavioral Examples Targeted for Team Leaders

Competency: **Technical Credibility**

Definition: Understands and appropriately applies principles, procedures, requirements, regulations, and policies related to specialized expertise

Behavioral Examples for the Team Leader Role

- Assesses expertise of team members in relation to the needs of the team project and seeks expertise outside the team when needed.

- Demonstrates knowledge of basic concepts, facts, and principles of particular subject matter domain and continues to develop expertise.

- Presents results of team project to the larger work unit.

- Seeks information on procedures, regulations, and policies that will affect the team project and keeps team members informed of this information.

- Seeks skills, knowledge, and abilities in maintaining and building own team of expertise.

- Presents information to others in area of expertise.

- Effectively leverages the varied types of technical expertise within the team.

Behavioral Examples for Team Leaders

Competency: **Accountability**

Definition: Holds self and others accountable for measurable high-quality, timely, and cost-effective results. Determines objectives, sets priorities, and delegates work. Accepts responsibility for mistakes. Complies with established control systems and rules.

Behavioral Examples for the Team Leader Role

- Demonstrates ability to translate stakeholder mandates into effective strategies and achievable programs of action.

- Holds team and project members accountable for achieving results within assigned deadlines.

- Listens to experts and balances various assessments of risk before making decisions of critical importance.

- Maintains good overview and control of project/group budgets and costs.

- Prioritizes team/project tasks with respect to importance and time available while maintaining short- and long-term focus on task completion.

- Seeks the input of legal and ethical advisors when not clear how such framework must be applied in a given context.

- Takes personal responsibility for team/group outcomes.

- Understands, and is able to work within, the legal and ethical framework constraints of the workplace.

Behavioral Examples for Team Leaders

Competency: **Conflict Management**

Definition: Encourages creative tension and differences of opinions. Anticipates and takes steps to prevent counterproductive confrontations. Manages and resolves conflicts and disagreements in a constructive manner.

Behavioral Examples for the Team Leader Role

- Addresses disagreements among team members in a constructive manner by remaining calm and focusing on the information rather than the emotion.

- Establishes a team environment that invites multiple views and perspectives as a basic operating principle.

- Demonstrates skill in informal facilitation of conflict resolution.

- Knows team members well enough to sense which situations might generate disagreement.

- Practices skilled listening.

- Requests team members discuss differences interfering with team creativity, cohesiveness, and productivity.

- Demonstrates skill in facilitating group discussions.

- Treats all members of the team with respect.

Behavioral Examples for Team Leaders

Competency: **Continual Learning**

Definition: Assesses and recognizes own strengths and weaknesses. Pursues self-development.

Behavioral Examples for the Team Leader Role

- Brings the most up-to-date technical information to the team and supports team members in doing so.

- Builds continual learning to collectively reflect on team progress, achievements, successes, and missteps.

- Draws on individual team member strengths rather than weaknesses to fashion assignments and help develop others in the team.

- Shows insight into individuals' learning profiles and styles when making assignments or devising developmental strategies.

- Supports the team's use of a variety of learning methods, including reading, talking with others, after-action reviews, attending formal training, and on-the-job experiences.

- Uses after-action reviews to assess performance.

Behavioral Examples for Team Leaders

Competency: **Creativity and Innovation**

Definition: Develops new insights into situations. Questions conventional approaches. Encourages new ideas and innovations. Designs and implements new or cutting-edge programs/processes.

Behavioral Examples for the Team Leader Role

- Actively recruits for diversity of thought, talent, and perspective among team members.

- Effectively conducts creative problem-solving sessions with a team.

- Establishes team processes and strategies that look beyond traditional boundaries, ideas, and approaches.

- Facilitates team roles and processes that take greatest advantage of creative talent and innovative thought.

- Identifies issues and opportunities to improve team processes, products, services, and service delivery.

- Models creative thinking, problem solving.

- Sets high expectations for continuing improvements to processes, products, and services.

- Works with other teams, work units, and disciplines to achieve broader perspective on issues and to build on the good work of others.

Behavioral Examples for Team Leaders

Competency: **Cross-Cultural Interactions**

Definition: Interacts with people of other cultures with ease. Communicates and performs over distance, culture, and time differences. Understands the impact of culture on management strategy and style.

Behavioral Examples for the Team Leader Role

- Takes time zones into account when scheduling for meetings.

- Preparing for interactions by knowing what the language of the other person is and having resources, if needed, such as documents in their native language, interpreters, and other language supports.

- Ensures that all team members know how to access translation services if needed (such was when working with customers or stakeholders who do not speak a common language).

- Assesses the customer population to determine what culturally-appropriate products and services to offer.

- Takes time to build trust with and among team members, focusing on shared values and vision dedicated to executing the team's mission in support of the larger organization.

Behavioral Examples for Team Leaders

Competency: **Customer Service**

Definition: Anticipates and meets the needs of both internal and external customers. Delivers high-quality products and services. Demonstrates commitment to continuous improvement.

Behavioral Examples for the Team Leader Role

- Applies emerging ideas, innovations, and new technologies to serving the customer.

- Communicates a clear understanding of client needs and makes these central to decision making and service delivery.

- Designs customer feedback mechanisms into projects.

- Designs customer-friendly processes and procedures.

- Identifies and acts on opportunities to enhance customer service delivery systems.

- Regularly, clearly, and enthusiastically communicates to team members high expectations for good customer service.

- Researches and addresses underlying customer needs. Goes beyond the obvious and the most expedient when in the best long-term interest of the customer.

- Uses legal and ethical standards to help resolve issues of fairness, equality, and appropriate scope of services and approaches.

Behavioral Examples for Team Leaders

Competency: **Developing Others**

Definition: Develops the ability of others to perform and contribute to the organization by providing ongoing feedback and by providing opportunities to learn through formal and informal methods.

Behavioral Examples for the Team Leader Role

- Builds team skills through assignments, coaching, and training related both to task accomplishment as well as to relationship building and group processes.

- Discusses team and individual training needs with Supervisors.

- Gives feedback to the group as a whole and/or to individual group members in a way that enables positive performance change.

- Identifies potential training opportunities for team members that would assist with successful completion of team projects.

- Passes on information learned in own training opportunities to team members.

- Provides opportunities for team members to share skills and knowledge that will aid in the completion of team projects.

- Recognizes and addresses team and team member strengths and developing needs in knowledge and performance.

Behavioral Examples for Team Leaders

Competency: **Entrepreneurship**

Definition: Positions the organization for future success by identifying new opportunities. Builds the organization by developing or improving products or services. Takes calculated risks to accomplish organizational objectives.

Behavioral Examples for the Team Leader Role

- Encourages team members to make innovative suggestions and to try new approaches.

- Demonstrates openness toward new approaches and ideas, is supportive of risk taking.

- Helps team members find ways to circumvent obstacles.

- Maintains an "outcomes" orientation. Demonstrates willingness to try many different approaches and processes to achieve desired outcomes.

- Makes best use of diverse talents, technology, and resources to deliver results. Builds on employees' strengths.

- Recognizes and accepts risk of failure in suggesting and developing modifications to products or service delivery.

- Recognizes and informs supervisor of the innovative suggestions of team members.

- Suggests and initiates modifications to specific products or service delivery options to achieve the organization's mission.

Behavioral Examples for Team Leaders

Competency: **External Awareness**

Definition: Understands and keeps up to date on local, national, and international policies and trends that affect the organization and shape stakeholders' views. Demonstrates awareness of the organization's impact on the external environment

Behavioral Examples for the Team Leader Role

- Collects data and performs analyses (such as technology forecasting, decision analysis, and statistical models) on current and potential conditions, and facilitates an understanding of external activities on organizational actions.

- Communicates a clear understanding of internal and external client needs; makes these central to decision making and service delivery.

- Communicates to all team members the impact of Agency policies and priorities on the team's area of work and the customers with whom they work.

- Demonstrates an understanding of the national policy-making and implementation processes.

- Flexibly redirects project and team processes to maintain alignment with organizational direction.

- Keeps abreast of key organizational policies and priorities likely to affect the program area.

- When representing the organization, demonstrates sensitivity to the political, social, and cultural nuances of issues.

Behavioral Examples for Team Leaders

Competency: **Financial Management**

Definition: Understands the organization's financial processes. Prepares, justifies, and administers the program budget. Oversees procurement and contracting to achieve desired results. Monitors expenditures and uses cost-benefit thinking to set priorities.

Behavioral Examples for the Team Leader Role

- Ensures appropriate oversight and control over procurement and contracting.

- Ensures all team members involved in these activities have adequate training to prepare them for competent and ethical performance and accountability.

- Estimates the type and level of resources needed for team to meet its goals under the Agency's strategic plan.

- Investigates ways to use more cost-effective means to accomplish team project goals.

- Matches customer needs to available services, budget, and resources.

- Monitors, reviews, and tracks expenditures and other resource use related to operations, including personnel, overtime, supplies, and equipment.

- Proactively seeks the necessary project resources through careful planning and articulate, compelling justification.

- Uses budget and financial reports to determine if project is fiscally on target.

Behavioral Examples for Team Leaders

Competency: **Flexibility**

Definition: Demonstrates openness to change and new information. Rapidly adapts to new information, changing conditions, or unexpected obstacles.

Behavioral Examples for the Team Leader Role

- Adapts team interaction and communication styles to fit with style preferences of team members.

- Adjusts team members' workload and tasks when other work or personal responsibilities require.

- Encourages team to employ a variety of techniques for exploring different options.

- Simultaneously handles multiple projects and duties, prioritizing as needed.

- Helps individual team members find their balance in new, ambiguous, and more demanding circumstances to circumvent obstacles.

- Modifies team assignments, when feasible, to take advantage of individual strengths.

- Suggests different approaches for customers with diverse needs.

- Treats each person according to his or her unique makeup, instilling mutual understanding, trust, and confidence.

Behavioral Examples for Team Leaders

Competency: **Human Capital Management**

Definition: Builds and manages workforce based on organizational goals, budget considerations, and staffing needs. Ensures employees are appropriately recruited, selected, appraised, and rewarded. Takes action to address performance problems. Manage a multi-sector workforce and a variety of work situations.

Behavioral Examples for the Team Leader Role

- Advises supervisor on performance of team members.

- Advises supervisor if additional human resources are needed for project success.

- Communicates with supervisor on developmental needs of individual team members and/or additional staffing needs to complete team project.

- Makes suggestions to supervisor on recognition methods for individual or team accomplishments.

- Notifies supervisor if performance problems arise among team members requiring supervisory assistance to resolve.

- Recognizes and addresses team and team member strengths and potential "fatal flaws" in knowledge and performance.

- Understands the concept of "Human Capital" and treats team members as valuable assets.

- Understands the goals and strategies of the organization and can link team's task, and current skills, knowledge, and abilities to these long-range and larger vision.

Behavioral Examples for Team Leaders

Competency: **Integrity and Honesty**

Definition: Behaves in an honest, fair, and ethical manner. Shows consistency in words and actions. Creates a culture that fosters high ethical standards.

Behavioral Examples for the Team Leader Role

- Brings in expert sources to help clarify issues, legal requirements, and thought processes in ethical decisions.
- Refuses to sacrifice trust and integrity to expediency, even under pressure. Refuses to make inappropriate decisions for personal gain, to include career advancements.
- Ensures the integrity of accounting and performance data through good data collection and analysis systems.
- Holds team members accountable for issues of integrity, honesty, and duty.
- Maintains confidentiality and protects the privacy of employees, customers, and other members of the public.
- Models personal and professional integrity in actions.
- Offers honest, useful feedback and identifies people's needs for development.
- Understands the legal and ethical framework of the civil service and does not transgress against it, even when it might seem to offer some benefit to the project or program.

Behavioral Examples for Team Leaders

Competency: **Interpersonal Skills**

Definition: Treats others with courtesy, sensitivity, and respect. Considers and appropriately responds to the needs and feelings of different people in different situations.

Behavioral Examples for the Team Leader Role

- Defers judgment on what someone is saying and focuses instead on learning more.

- Helps the team set norms it can live by and that encourage respect, participation, and trust.

- Demonstrates skillful facilitating of group processes; possesses an intrinsic understanding of what is happening in a group and when to intervene.

- Demonstrates sensitivity to the needs of those who perceive offense.

- Mentors team members on how to collaboratively work with others.

- Promotes an atmosphere of confidence and trust and builds a team characterized by trust, involvement, and empowerment.

- Recognizes and capitalizes on opportunities for members of workgroups and teams to understand each other and to develop a mutually supportive environment.

- Treats all members of the team with respect.

Behavioral Examples for Team Leaders

Competency: **Leveraging Diversity**

Definition: Fosters an inclusive workplace where diversity and individual differences are valued and leveraged to achieve the vision and mission of the organization.

Behavioral Examples for the Team Leader Role

- Capitalizes on team members' strengths and differences to contribute to organizational and individual development and effectiveness.

- Considers customers' special needs when developing and implementing programs, such as bilingual or bicultural services.

- Creates a safe environment for difference.

- Develops a culture of inclusiveness, respect, and civility that values difference.

- Exercises authority, when necessary, to maintain civility, inclusiveness, and fairness.

- Seeks member diversity when building a team.

- Identifies the forces shaping the views and actions of clients, customers, or competitors.

- Identifies the implications of the MBTI and similar tools for team work and can use these differences to enhance the team's success.

Behavioral Examples for Team Leaders

Competency: **Oral Communication**

Definition: Makes clear and convincing oral presentations. Listens effectively. Clarifies information as needed. Facilitates open communication.

Behavioral Examples for the Team Leader Role

- Encourages team members to express their opinions, ideas, and concerns and listens empathetically.

- Helps team members learn to communicate in productive ways with each other and with other units or groups.

- Facilitates and uses strategies drawing more reticent team members into the discussion.

- Listens to team members and responds appropriately.

- Makes effective presentations on team projects and responds clearly and effectively to questions about the team project.

- Takes into account the impact of emotions and feelings on a situation.

- Employs communication as a strategic issue, anticipating and responding to the needs of all affected groups, including team members.

- Effectively uses various channels of communication, including meetings, briefings, and the media.

Behavioral Examples for Team Leaders

Competency: **Partnering**

Definition: Develops networks and builds alliances. Collaborates across boundaries to build strategic relationships and achieve common goals.

Behavioral Examples for the Team Leader Role

- Actively brings the team together with other groups to find common solutions to similar problems.

- Builds collaborative relationships with team members and customers.

- Helps others get beyond turf issues by emphasizing the benefits of collaboration.

- Develops and uses networks with appropriate individuals or groups within or outside the Agency.

- Discovers and shares appropriate information to assist team in achieving its goals.

- Manages competition among team members to eliminate barriers to building partnerships.

- Reaches out to provide information and assistance to others across organizational lines.

- Demonstrates collaborative leadership and possesses good facilitation skills.

Behavioral Examples for Team Leaders

Competency: **Political Savvy**

Definition: Identifies the internal and external politics impacting the work of the organization. Perceives organizational and political reality and acts accordingly.

Behavioral Examples for the Team Leader Role

- Builds lateral support for initiatives; mobilizes the support of others whose cooperation, backing, and/or approval is required.
- Determines which people are critical to accomplishing results and brings them together.
- Effectively influences workgroups and units outside span of control using practices that reinforce understanding of mutual interests and support continuing collaborative endeavors.
- Keeps supervisor and other key organizational personnel informed of important decisions and changes on team projects.
- Recognizes when to compromise and when to remain firm to accomplish broader organizational objectives affecting the team.
- Manages the interrelationships between own unit and the major functions within the larger organization, such as finance, information, and human resources; effectively works with each in planning, implementing, and sustaining the unit's work.
- Identifies underlying sources and issues behind constituent needs and provides service that best attempts to address them.
- Broadly works with stakeholders to create a shared vision, balancing and reconciling various interests.

Behavioral Examples for Team Leaders

Competency: **Problem Solving**

Definition: Identifies and analyzes problems. Weighs relevance and accuracy of information. Generates and evaluates alternative solutions. Makes recommendations.

Behavioral Examples for the Team Leader Role

- States the problem in terms of needs, rather than solutions.
- Creates a team culture welcoming and employing new perspectives and ideas.
- Encourages team members to seek alternative solutions when a planned process or procedure is not working.
- Habitually explores multiple, sometimes unconventional, options and different perspectives in order to gain the best solution.
- Helps team members understand and evaluate complex situations and ideas, frame problems clearly, and sort out symptoms from root cause.
- Imbues team culture with openness to alternatives. Establishes team processes and strategies that look beyond traditional boundaries, ideas, and approaches.
- Seeks input from customers, coworkers, and other stakeholders when the team project is to resolve a problem or improve a process.
- Identifies patterns or trends; links parts of a problem to a broader set of issues or relationships.
- Uses collaborative problem-solving skills to generate solutions.

Behavioral Examples for Team Leaders

Competency: **Resilience**

Definition: Effectively deals with pressure. Remains optimistic and persistent, even under adversity. Quickly recovers from setback.

Behavioral Examples for the Team Leader Role

- Focuses work unit efforts on handling challenges by helping employees identify what they can do to overcome challenges.

- Optimistically presents information to encourage acceptance by members of the workgroup, yet honestly gives worst-case scenarios when appropriate.

- Focuses on what was learned from and can be done to prevent setbacks.

- Models behavior helping people maintain focus and effectiveness during change.

- Remains alert to and able to recognize signs of stress as it impacts productivity, teamwork, and creativity.

- Understands how a positive, supportive work environment promotes higher productivity throughout the organization.

- Utilizes effective time management for self and others (short, well-planned meetings etc.).

- Encourages cross-training on the team in order to build depth for times of crisis when additional trained personnel are required.

Behavioral Examples for Team Leaders

Competency: **Strategic Thinking**

Definition: Formulates objectives and priorities, and implements plans consistent with the long-term interests of the organization in a global environment. Capitalizes on opportunities and manages risk.

Behavioral Examples for the Team Leader Role

- Anticipates new or changed demands for programs and services and leads team in seeking information to guide action.

- Applies an understanding of past situations to anticipate and deal with threats and opportunities to team project accomplishment.

- Organizes resources and activities to deal with longer-term problems or opportunities.

- Recognizes individual and workgroup contributions to enhancements of organizational performance.

- Seeks ideas and information from team members on possible enhancements or impediments to organizational performance.

- Takes the initiative to understand team activity from the customer's viewpoint.

Behavioral Examples for Team Leaders

Competency: **Technology Management**

Definition: Keeps up to date on technological developments. Makes effective use of technology to achieve results. Ensures access to and security of technology system.

Behavioral Examples for the Team Leader Role

- Considers customers' access to technology in team project design.

- Identifies lessons learned from successful and unsuccessful Information Technology (IT) projects and builds on these in new projects.

- Keeps up to date with technologies that might enhance team communication and other group processes.

- Partners with technology professionals to ensure optimal and cost-effective technology support to programs, processes, and services.

- Requests technology and training as needed to accomplish team projects.

- Uses technology to facilitate access to and sharing of information for the delivery of services to customers.

- Uses technology to improve team productivity.

Behavioral Examples for Team Leaders

Competency: **Vision**

Definition: Takes a long-term view and builds a shared vision with others. Acts as a catalyst for organizational change. Influences others to translate vision into action.

Behavioral Examples for the Team Leader Role

- Stays abreast of changes in organizational goals, objectives, and initiatives.

- Understands organizational direction and ensures team contribution toward organizational goals and objectives.

- Helps individual team members find their balance in new, ambiguous, and more demanding circumstances.

- Restates goals, or establishes new ones, as changing circumstances require.

- Communicates changing organizational context and relates to team/project.

- Provides feedback on team's contribution to organizational objectives.

- Sets clear short- and long-term objectives for teams and projects.

- Uses Agile precepts to drive team performance.

Behavioral Examples for Team Leaders

Competency: **Written Communication**

Definition: Writes in a clear, concise, organized, and convincing manner for the intended audience.

Behavioral Examples for the Team Leader Role

- Determines when graphics, charts, and sketches are needed to support and clarify text.

- Ensures the team understands and effectively and appropriately uses electronic and written communication.

- Issues information via the appropriate medium, such as e-mail, hard copy memos, and organizational instructions.

- Conveys the legal and regulatory requirements clearly and concisely in written communications.

- Adheres to organizational guidelines use of email and other electronic to update supervisors and stakeholders of team/project process.

- Writes in a way that makes complex technical concepts understandable.

- Writes team project reports, correspondence, assessments, and other documents clearly, succinctly, and for the intended audience.

Chapter 5:
Leadership Development for Supervisors

Primary focus:
   Leading People

Core Competencies:
   - Accountability
   - Conflict Management
   - Developing Others
   - Human Capital Management
   - Leveraging Diversity

Leadership Role Continuum
All Employees --> Team Leader --> **Supervisor** --> Manager --> Executive

---

Are you in a supervisor role or want to be in a supervisor role? The following pages spell out the leadership competencies and the behavioral examples for the role of supervisor.

Follow the process as outlined in Chapter 2:

1. Identify your goal
2. Assess proficiency
3. Identify learning experiences
4. Create your development plan
5. Complete learning experiences
6. Assess progress
7. Repeat

As you work though your development plan, review the behavioral examples on the following pages. These examples should provide you with a fairly comprehensive view of what the leadership competencies look like for the role of supervisor.

Behavioral Examples Targeted for Supervisors

Competency: **Accountability**

Definition: Holds self and others accountable for measurable high-quality, timely, and cost-effective results. Determines objectives, sets priorities, and delegates work. Accepts responsibility for mistakes. Complies with established control systems and rules.

Behavioral Examples for the Supervisor Role

- Creates/maintains a supportive environment for internal control systems against fraud, waste, and mismanagement.
- Defines, communicates, and measures progress against rigorous outcome criteria for successful performance.
- Evaluates workgroup performance and project accomplishment to assess overall program effectiveness and efficiency.
- Identifies potential problems in employee behavior and takes appropriate action within organizational guidelines.
- Keeps managers informed of valuable lessons learned, as well as project results.
- Maintains good overview and control of contract performance.
- Prepares project and work unit plans with short- and long-range measurable objectives.
- Uses results-oriented performance measures -- such as quantity, cost, timeliness, and quality of products or services -- in assessing outcomes.

Behavioral Examples Targeted for Supervisors

Competency: **Conflict Management**

Definition: Encourages creative tension and differences of opinions. Anticipates and takes steps to prevent counterproductive confrontations. Manages and resolves conflicts and disagreements in a constructive manner.

Behavioral Examples for the Supervisor Role

- Actively involves employees and team or work unit in resolving differences over work issues, such as schedules, assignments, and ensuring employee and organizational concerns are balanced.
- Actively listens to the concerns of employees regarding issues such as organizational changes, quality of work life, and other issues that might cause employees worry or stress.
- Anticipates the range of reactions that typically occur when change is introduced.
- Holds staff accountable for avoiding and resolving conflicts.
- Is knowledgeable of appropriate policies and procedures in dealing with conflicts.
- Recognizes potential for violence and sabotage in the workplace and takes preventive action to address problems with troubled employees.
- Refers complex conflicts and others not amenable to informal resolution to mediation specialists.
- Seeks input of employees through their representative associations or union officials to address matters that affect them in the workplace.
- Takes preventive action to assure on-the-job safety and security of employees.

Behavioral Examples Targeted for Supervisors

Competency: **Developing Others**

Definition: Develops the ability of others to perform and contribute to the organization by providing ongoing feedback and by providing opportunities to learn through formal and informal methods.

Behavioral Examples for the Supervisor Role

- Defines, clearly communicates, and measures progress against rigorous outcome criteria for successful performance.
- Encourages the use of self-assessments, assessments by others, and performance evaluations to identify employee training needs.
- Ensures development resources are fairly distributed among employees.
- Ensures IDPs are in place for all employees, linking individual development with Agency mission and strategic needs.
- Provides employees with ongoing feedback on areas of strength and needed development.
- Provides one-on-one time for each employee focusing on his or her development.
- Reinforces knowledge, skills, and new behaviors gained through training and development by helping employees apply these on the job.
- Supports the development of individuals and encourages them to take responsibility for their own development.

Behavioral Examples Targeted for Supervisors

Competency: **Human Capital Management**

Definition: Builds and manages workforce based on organizational goals, budget considerations, and staffing needs. Ensures employees are appropriately recruited, selected, appraised, and rewarded. Takes action to address performance problems. Manages a multi-sector workforce and a variety of work situations.

Behavioral Examples for the Supervisor Role

- Delegates work and assigns projects designed to strengthen employee knowledge, skills, and abilities.
- Follows merit principles when selecting, developing, utilizing, appraising, and rewarding employees.
- Fosters a culture of trust, respect, teamwork, communication, creativity, equal opportunity, and empowerment.
- Involves labor partners in formulating new human resource practices.
- Provides resources employees need to effectively perform their tasks, including special accommodations.
- Recognizes and rewards employees based on effective performance.
- Takes timely and forthright action to counsel, discipline, or remove employees as performance or conduct problems arise.
- Understands the concept of "Human Capital" and treats people as valuable assets.
- Works to meet people where they are, realizing that every individual is unique and brings their own strengths to the job.

Behavioral Examples Targeted for Supervisors

Competency: **Leveraging Diversity**

Definition: Fosters an inclusive workplace where diversity and individual differences are valued and lever- aged to achieve the vision and mission of the organization.

Behavioral Examples for the Supervisor Role

- Develops a culture of inclusiveness, respect, and civility that values differences.
- Develops and implements plans for assessing and dealing with concerns and needs of persons with disabilities and considers such things as technology, equipment, space, interpreters, and door openers.
- Ensures subordinates have training that helps them understand others' perspectives.
- Helps others to see new possibilities. Challenges employees to take a different perspective.
- Holds employees accountable for ensuring equality and diversity within work units.
- Monitors, evaluates, and promotes broad-based diversity as a means to leverage the full range of human potential and performance.
- Proactively works with program officials to develop and implement effective recruitment, retention, and upward mobility programs building diversity and significantly improving organizational performance.
- Works with union officials and other stakeholders to identify and remove obstacles to understanding and to encourage a positive workplace culture.

Behavioral Examples for Supervisors

Competency: **Continual Learning**

Definition: Assesses and recognizes own strengths and weaknesses. Pursues self-development.

Behavioral Examples for the Supervisor Role

- Contributes to procedures that enable the organization to learn from past actions.

- Invests in the further development of own supervisory skills; in better understanding the issues and needs that affect customers and in own field- specific expertise.

- Knows and accesses training resources inside and outside the organization for the benefit of individuals in the unit.

- Measures current skills and knowledge against competencies needed for continuing success and to meet future problems.

- Provides one-on-one time for each employee focused on her or his development.

- Uses a variety of approaches to analyze and understand how actions lead to certain outcomes and how to improve one's approach to similar situations in the future.

Behavioral Examples for Supervisors

Competency: **Creativity and Innovation**

Definition: Develops new insights into situations. Questions conventional approaches. Encourages new ideas and innovations. Designs and implements new or cutting edge systems, processes, products, or services.

Behavioral Examples for the Supervisor Role

- Allows and encourages creative, innovative, and nonconventional contributions, even when this leads to conflict.

- Communicates a personal commitment to continual organizational improvement.

- Encourages employees to find creative ways to save time and cost.

- Establishes staffing strategies and work processes encouraging the consideration of multiple approaches and nonconventional thought.

- Invests in training for team/unit members enabling employees to weigh potential solutions and initiatives for appropriateness and feasibility.

- Models creative thinking and problem solving.

- Routinely develops and weighs alternatives before settling on a solution.

- Understands the role of evaluation and testing in creative processes.

Behavioral Examples for Supervisors

Competency: **Cross-Cultural Interactions**

Definition: Interacts with people of other cultures with ease. Communicates and performs over distance, culture, and time differences. Understands the impact of culture on management strategy and style.

Behavioral Examples for the Supervisor Role

- Acknowledges cultural differences and works to supervise all employees with equity.

- Uses the LEARN acronym in ensuring clear two-way, cross-cultural communication: Listen, Effectively communicate, Avoid ambiguity, Respect differences, No judgement.

- Reviews standard practices to ensure certain cultures are not treated differently systemically.

- Endeavors to create an environment respectful of the diversity of cultures, celebrating not the differences between us but the uniqueness of what makes us human.

- Forges a common vision based around mission and values that transcends cultural differences.

Behavioral Examples for Supervisors

Competency: **Customer Service**

Definition: Anticipates and meets the needs of both internal and external customers. Delivers high-quality products and services. Demonstrates commitment to continuous improvement.

Behavioral Examples for the Supervisor Role

- Acts promptly to prevent customer complaints from having negative impact on reaching goals.

- Builds knowledge from past experiences into decision-making process.

- Communicates decisions made and the rationale behind them.

- Delegates authority and responsibility to others who may be closer to the problem.

- Seeks legal and ethical advice when questions of this nature arise, or actions to be taken are unclear.

- Understands operational implications of strategy and can look beyond solutions that are merely expedient.

- Institutes methods of gathering customer feedback on provided services.

Behavioral Examples for Supervisors

Competency: **Decisiveness**

Definition: Makes effective and timely decisions, even when data is limited or solutions produce unpleasant consequences. Perceives the impact and implications of decisions.

Behavioral Examples for the Supervisor Role

- Ensures decisions are aligned with and support the organization's mission, vision, and strategic goals.

- Makes sound, timely decisions for the work unit regarding technical approaches, methods, work processes, staff, equipment, facilities, or funds.

- Recognizes and resolves controversy before it creates an adverse effect on the organizational unit, such as resolving conflict over workload distribution or work schedules.

- Recognizes early warning signs and opportunities, and takes action.

- Recognizes opportunities for individual and organizational growth and takes action.

- Takes immediate corrective action when needed, for example, terminating a contract due to lack of timeliness, poor quality, or cost increases.

- Knows when information is sufficient for decision making.

Behavioral Examples for Supervisors

Competency: **Entrepreneurship**

Definition: Positions the organization for future success by identifying new opportunities. Builds the organization by developing or improving products or services. Takes calculated risks to accomplish organizational objectives.

Behavioral Examples for the Supervisor Role

- Actively partners with other units to improve products, services, delivery, and to enhance cost effectiveness.

- Encourages employees to make innovative suggestions and to try new approaches within the workgroup.

- Provides structures for trying new ideas and rewards for innovation.

- Recognizes and accepts risk of failure in suggesting and developing modifications to products or service delivery.

- Recognizes and rewards employees who make innovative suggestions that improve work unit processes, procedures, environment, and customer service.

- Suggests and initiates modifications to specific products or service delivery options to increase market potential.

- Supports and communicates the role diversity plays in innovation throughout the unit.

- Demonstrates a willingness to initiate change.

Behavioral Examples for Supervisors

Competency: **External Awareness**

Definition: Understands and keeps up to date on local, national, and international policies and trends that affect the organization and shape stakeholders' views. Demonstrates awareness of the organization's impact on the external environment.

Behavioral Examples for the Supervisor Role

- Encourages others to see the big picture by demonstrating how various internal and external functions interrelate.

- Demonstrates knowledge of and maintains a current understanding of the larger organizational culture, the interrelationships forming it, and how one's own activities (team, unit, organization, and nation) fit into it.

- Maintains contacts with external customers and stakeholders through various communication channels.

- Recognizes the impact on stakeholders of alternate courses of action.

- Recognizes the interdependencies of all organizational units and collaborates to maximize resources, share information, and synergize outcomes.

- Understands the organization's process systems and information flow.

- Understands underlying sources and issues behind constituent needs and provides service that best attempts to address them, going beyond the obvious and the most expedient to focus on long-term results.

Behavioral Examples for Supervisors

Competency: **Financial Management**

Definition: Understands the organization's financial processes. Prepares, justifies, and administers the program budget. Oversees procurement and contracting to achieve desired results. Monitors expenditures and uses cost-benefit thinking to set priorities.

Behavioral Examples for the Supervisor Role

- Prepares and justifies budget for organizational unit or project activities.

- Constructs an accurate and compelling business case for a project.

- Ensures appropriate oversight and control over procurement and contracting.

- Ensures that employees involved in finance-related activities have adequate training to prepare them for competent and ethical performance and accountability.

- Estimates the type and level of resources needed for team/unit to meet its goals under the organization's strategic plan.

- Identifies cost-effective approaches.

- Monitors, reviews, and tracks expenditures and other resource use related to operations, including personnel, overtime, supplies, and equipment.

- Understands and applies the organization's systems of resource allocation.

Behavioral Examples for Supervisors

Competency: **Flexibility**

Definition: Demonstrates openness to change and new information. Rapidly adapts to new information, changing conditions, or unexpected obstacles.

Behavioral Examples for the Supervisor Role

- Adapts supervisory style to individual needs of employees.
- Applies change management principles (including understanding the change involved, differentiating between change and transition, handling resistance, handling group dynamics, using systems approaches, articulating the benefits of the change for individuals and the organization) to implement change in work unit.
- Effectively and strategically delegates in response to change or crisis.
- Fosters flexibility through cross-training and developmental assignments.
- Keeps employees informed of how their work effort is related to the change; and how they will be expected to participate in the new effort.
- Recognizes when a situation calls for, or could benefit from, a different approach.
- Responds to differing circumstances and individual customer and employee needs.
- Adapts own leadership style to the occasion.
- Uses flexible systems enabling better work/life balance.
- Promotes flexibility in service delivery in order to equitably serve all customers.

Behavioral Examples for Supervisors

Competency: **Influencing and Negotiating**

Definition: Persuades others. Builds consensus through give and take. Gains cooperation from others to obtain information and accomplish goals

Behavioral Examples for the Supervisor Role

- Builds consensus among groups or individuals with differing interests and opinions to solve problems or make decisions.
- Effectively employs a variety of negotiation techniques, allowing differing parties to reach mutually agreeable solutions.
- Effectively influences workgroups and units outside span of control using practices that both reinforce understanding of mutual interests and support continuing collaborative endeavors.
- In communicating change, uses compelling vision, clear and detailed steps, and persuasive skills to help people realign their work and energy.
- Influences unit's performance through effective feedback, coaching, counseling, and mentoring.
- Successfully negotiates with internal groups to facilitate programs or partnerships.
- Uses clear, persuasive, attention getting, and accurate communication to make others aware of the issues, to help others envision the goals, and to gain buy-in.
- Uses collaboration across functions and units to extend influence throughout the system where they have no formal authority.

Behavioral Examples for Supervisors

Competency: **Integrity and Honesty**

Definition: Behaves in an honest, fair, and ethical manner. Shows consistency in words and actions. Creates a culture that fosters high ethical standards.

Behavioral Examples for the Supervisor Role

- Creates a climate that supports integrity and honesty in the organization, through personal example but also through processes and procedures that reward and encourage ethical behavior.
- Refuses to sacrifice trust and integrity to expediency, even under pressure. Refuses to make inappropriate decisions for personal gain, to include career advancements.
- Ensures all employees have adequate training to prepare them for competent and ethical performance.
- Holds employees accountable for issues of integrity, honesty, and duty.
- Instills a climate of trust by keeping one's word and taking responsibility for one's actions.
- Maintains confidentiality and protects the privacy of employees, customers, and other members of the public.
- Makes decisions and the thinking behind them transparent to those affected by them.
- Prohibits retaliatory actions against employees who raise ethical issues, speaking out against abuses.
- Understands the legal and ethical framework system within which they operate and maintains trust and integrity even under pressure.

Behavioral Examples for Supervisors

Competency: **Interpersonal Skills**

Definition: Treats others with courtesy, sensitivity, and respect. Considers and appropriately responds to the needs and feelings of different people in different situations.

Behavioral Examples for the Supervisor Role

- Coaches, teaches, counsels, and motivates employees toward greater mutual respect and understanding.

- Confronts performance problems in a way that maintains a positive relationship.

- Ensures subordinates have training that helps them to understand the perspective of others.

- Fosters an atmosphere where subordinates are able to voice their concerns or ideas without fear of criticism, ridicule, or retaliation.

- Invites contact and is easy to approach.

- Takes an appropriate personal interest in coworkers and employees to develop a healthy and productive working environment.

- Takes control of situations where subordinates are being subjected to undesirable or inappropriate behavior.

- Treats all employees with respect regardless of their level, personality, culture, or background.

Behavioral Examples for Supervisors

Competency: **Oral Communication**

Definition: Makes clear and convincing oral presentations. Listens effectively. Clarifies information as needed. Facilitates open communication.

Behavioral Examples for the Supervisor Role

- Effectively gains support for a position or proposal through persuasive discussion.
- Encourages employees to express their opinions, ideas, and concerns and empathetically listens.
- Helps others prepare for interviews, performance reviews, and other meetings to ensure the meetings yield common understandings and achieve strategic goals.
- Influences unit's performance through effective feedback, coaching, counseling, and mentoring.
- Demonstrates sensitivity to personal space, touch, and other cultural and individual differences that affect communication.
- Actively listens to others in personal discussion or in open employee forums and responds appropriately.
- Responds appropriately to challenging questions or comments.
- Skillfully probes and asks questions that help others reflect and create insight.
- Effectively communicates within a wide range of contexts.
- Maintains an even tone in moments of high tension; treats others with respect, even in times of crisis.

Behavioral Examples for Supervisors

Competency: **Partnering**

Definition: Develops networks and builds alliances. Collaborates across boundaries to build strategic relationships and achieve common goals.

Behavioral Examples for the Supervisor Role

- Builds collaborative relationships with employee groups, stakeholders, industry, and other organizations that help achieve work unit objectives.

- Creates opportunities and incentives to learn and share knowledge with others about partnering successes and opportunities.

- Develops and uses networks with appropriate individuals or groups within or outside the agency.

- Reaches out to provide information and assistance to others across organizational lines.

- Recognizes when assistance is needed and seeks assistance in accomplishing organizational objectives.

- Rewards active exploration of partnering possibilities.

- Shares innovative partnering ideas with others.

- Uses collaborative work initiatives to increase the coherence, strength, and effectiveness within the unit.

Behavioral Examples for Supervisors

Competency: **Political Savvy**

Definition: Identifies the internal and external politics impacting the work of the organization. Perceives organizational and political reality and acts accordingly.

Behavioral Examples for the Supervisor Role

- Builds lateral support for initiatives; mobilizes the support of others whose cooperation, backing, and/or approval is required.
- Determines which people are critical to accomplishing results and brings them together.
- Helps employees and those one is mentoring understand how to get ahead in the organization using strategies and tactics that are honorable and fair.
- Involves stakeholders in making decisions for work unit and gains their support.
- Keeps key organizational personnel and key stakeholders informed of important decisions concerning work unit and situations.
- Recognizes when to compromise and when to remain firm to accomplish broader organizational objectives affecting the work unit.
- Understands the interrelationships between own unit and the major functions within an Agency, such as finance, information technology, and human resources; works effectively with each in planning, implementing, and sustaining the work of the unit.
- Whenever possible, partners with the union as an influence strategy to build commitment.
- Broadly works with stakeholders to create a shared vision, balancing and reconciling various interests along the way.

Behavioral Examples for Supervisors

Competency: **Problem Solving**

Definition: Identifies and analyzes problems. Weighs relevance and accuracy of information. Generates and evaluates alternative solutions. Makes recommendations.

Behavioral Examples for the Supervisor Role

- Acts as troubleshooter by discovering and eliminating causes of organizational or employee problems.

- Asks for advice from others on the implications of any trade-off decisions needing to be made.

- Encourages employees to find ways to circumvent obstacles.

- Generates solutions to problems and takes appropriate action leading to resolution.

- Identifies the key issues and applies problem-solving techniques to issues of change.

- Investigates and analyzes the conditions that led to a problem, the actions taken for solution, and the relevant outcomes to identify lessons learned for preventive action.

- Looks for what can be done in response to problems rather than what can not; weighs alternatives before moving forward.

- Prioritizes among issues and problems, judging importance, feasibility, appropriateness, and consequences in selecting those to be addressed.

Behavioral Examples for Supervisors

Competency: **Resilience**

Definition: Effectively deals with pressure. Remains optimistic and persistent, even under adversity. Quickly recovers from setbacks.

Behavioral Examples for the Supervisor Role

- Assigns, directs, monitors, and appraises work in ways that respect the person; offers challenging but not threatening work assignments.

- Deals proactively with stress responses and behaviors within the group or team.

- Demonstrates concern for employees as individuals, not just workers.

- During change, assists peers and other members of the organizational unit to handle uncertainty and to persevere.

- Helps employees find a balance between home and office and implements programs that facilitate such balance.

- Maintains unit productivity, quality, and morale during change.

- Models assertive, positive attitudes and behaviors that foster a can-do atmosphere.

- Provides training and developmental opportunities that build a sense of capability.

- Remains alert to, and is able to recognize signs of stress as it impacts productivity, teamwork, and creativity.

Behavioral Examples for Supervisors

Competency: **Strategic Thinking**

Definition: Formulates objectives and priorities, and implements plans consistent with the long-term interests of the organization in a global environment. Capitalizes on opportunities and manages risk.

Behavioral Examples for the Supervisor Role

- Communicates performance expectations to employees making the link to organization's mission and strategic plan clear and compelling.

- Communicates the changes in processes, actions, and shorter-term goals required to maintain alignment of unit with longer-term objectives.

- Communicates to all employees how work unit activities and priorities relate to organizational strategic goals.

- Converts organization-wide strategies and policy direction into action items within areas of responsibility.

- Develops short- and long-term objectives for work plans that support strategic goals.

- Makes resource decisions supported by realistic strategic thinking.

- Reviews programs, processes, and progress, keeping alert to the need for modifications or reengineering.

- Suggests appropriate measures for assessing the work unit's contribution to the strategic plan.

Behavioral Examples for Supervisors

Competency: **Team Building**

Definition: Inspires and fosters team commitment, spirit, pride, and trust. Facilitates cooperation and motivates team members to accomplish group goals.

Behavioral Examples for the Supervisor Role

- Communicates and implements results of team efforts.

- Deals constructively with problems among employees or between teams.

- Invests in training for self and others that enhances group process, group management, and decision-making skills.

- Plans team membership to achieve the immediate task as well as to develop positive and ongoing working relationships spanning the organization.

- Recommends or approves formal recognition for work of the team.

- Selects team members who represent diverse interests, specialties, and technical expertise so as to have maximum leverage on the task.

- Selects team members who represent diverse interests, specialties, and skills in order to achieve organizational goals.

Behavioral Examples for Supervisors

Competency: **Technical Credibility**

Definition: Understands and appropriately applies principles, procedures, requirements, regulations, and policies related to specialized expertise.

Behavioral Examples for the Supervisor Role

- Explores environment for best practices and works to implement them.

- Involves staff in seeking to constantly improve work processes and outcomes.

- Regularly assesses work unit capability and helps build capability to support the organization's mission.

- Seeks information about new procedures, requirements, regulations, and policies and actively works to become an expert on matters relating to innovative solutions.

- Supports and encourages employees in maintaining and upgrading skills and knowledge related to assignments.

- Seeks feedback on effectiveness as a supervisor and actively develops own supervisory skills.

Behavioral Examples for Supervisors

Competency: **Technology Management**

Definition: Keeps up to date on technological developments. Makes effective use of technology to achieve results. Ensures access to and security of technology systems.

Behavioral Examples for the Supervisor Role

- Applies project management and capital project management skills in planning and implementing new technologies.

- Defines, communicates, and measures progress of IT projects against rigorous outcome criteria.

- Directs, controls, administers, regulates IT projects to ensure effectiveness related to organizational goals.

- Ensures computer security procedures are in place to protect integrity/confidentiality of records.

- Ensures employees acquire up-to-date technology skills by arranging for training and hands-on experience.

- Helps employees connect technological change with the Agency's goals and mission, and with their own contribution to that mission.

- Partners with technology professionals to ensure optimal and cost-effective technology support to programs, processes, and services.

- Uses technology to facilitate access to and sharing of information for the delivery of services to customers.

Behavioral Examples for Supervisors

Competency: **Vision**

Definition: Takes a long-term view and builds a shared vision with others. Acts as a catalyst for organizational change. Influences others to translate vision into action.

Behavioral Examples for the Supervisor Role

- Adapts rules, procedures, customs, and behaviors as required to support the organizational, program, and unit visions.

- Assists others to understand and handle the forces and opportunities that require changes of thought and approach.

- Helps staff members understand the context of their work and how it relates to the work of others.

- Moves organizational unit toward visionary goals through teamwork and collaboration using tools such as task forces, committees, focus groups, or special projects.

- Recognizes and rewards individual and workgroup contributions to visionary goals.

- Sets high expectations for continuing improvements to processes, products, and services.

- Supports and provides input to the core team involved in implementing the vision for the organization.

- Transforms visionary goals into actions for areas of responsibility.

Behavioral Examples for Supervisors

Competency: **Written Communication**

Definition: Writes in a clear, concise, organized, and convincing manner for the intended audience.

Behavioral Examples for the Supervisor Role

- Ensures staff understands and effectively and appropriately uses electronic and written communication.

- Issues information via the appropriate medium, such as email or an instant message platform or a hard copy memo.

- Uses a written style and vocabulary appropriate to the audience.

- Writes in a way that makes complex technical concepts understandable.

- Writes performance measures in a meaningful and understandable way for the employee, and with the technical accuracy that ensures they are measurable, verifiable, equitable, and achievable.

- Writes policies, issue papers, correspondence, program plans with clarity, succinctness, persuasiveness, and for the intended audience.

- Reports goals and accomplishments of work unit in clear and succinct manner.

Chapter 6:
Leadership Development for Managers

Primary focus:
  Managing Programs

Core Competencies:
- Creativity & Innovation
- Financial Management
- Partnering
- Political Savvy
- Strategic Thinking
- Technology Management

Leadership Role Continuum
All Employees --> Team Leader --> Supervisor --> **Manager** --> Executive

---

Are you in a manger role or want to be in a manager role? The following pages spell out the leadership competencies and the behavioral examples for the role of manager.

Follow the process as outlined in Chapter 2:

1. Identify your goal
2. Assess proficiency
3. Identify learning experiences
4. Create your development plan
5. Complete learning experiences
6. Assess progress
7. Repeat

As you work though your development plan, review the behavioral examples on the following pages. These examples should provide you with a fairly comprehensive view of what the leadership competencies look like for the role of manager.

Behavioral Examples Targeted for Managers

Competency: **Creativity and Innovation**

Definition: Develops new insights into situations. Questions conventional approaches. Encourages new ideas and innovations. Designs and implements new or cutting edge products, services, processes, or systems.

Behavioral Examples for the Manager Role

- Demonstrates willingness to test ideas and experiment; prepared to try different solutions approaches.
- Develops and maintains organizational climate, personnel, and structures that foster quick and creative responses to new situations.
- Develops strategies to attract and motivate superior employees with talent for creative and innovative thought.
- Demonstrates the ability to be agile and strategic in response to changing circumstances, priorities, and resources.
- Demonstrates alertness to emerging opportunities for improvement and a readiness to take advantage of them.
- Demonstrates openness to suggestions for improving work procedures, products, and services.
- Monitors the impact and success of new ideas and learns from their implementation.
- Broadly reaches out to other organizations, groups, and disciplines to solicit the ideas and perspectives of others in order to generate the best solutions.
- Sets aside funds for improvement initiatives and training in skills that foster creative thought and innovation.

Behavioral Examples Targeted for Managers

Competency: **Financial Management**

Definition: Understands the organization's financial processes. Prepares, justifies, and administers the organizational budget. Oversees procurement and contracting to achieve desired results. Monitors expenditures and uses cost-benefit thinking to set priorities.

Behavioral Examples for the Manager Role

- Ensures expenditure tracking, compliance with spending targets, and appropriate administrative control of funds.
- Assures appropriate oversight and control over procurement and contracting.
- Possesses an understanding of the drivers of costs and works to eliminate waste and inefficiency.
- Includes adequate funding for business training for key personnel in budget plans.
- Manages value for cost (return on investments) while working within a constrained financial regime.
- Monitors progress on budgetary goals, evaluates results, and reallocates as necessary.
- Reallocates resources throughout the organization as necessary to enhance program impact.
- Uses and can develop an annual business plan for the unit linking strategic outcomes with budgets and key operational metrics.
- Makes budget consolidation and reallocation decisions and can justify program budgets based on how programs fit into the organization's mission.

Behavioral Examples Targeted for Managers

Competency: **Partnering**

Definition: Develops networks and builds alliances. Collaborates across boundaries to build strategic relationships and achieve common goals.

Behavioral Examples for the Manager Role

- Ensures rigorous evaluation processes to measure the success of partnership efforts; compares results with expectations and analyzes how partnerships can be improved.

- Ensures all who are affected by the work of the partnership are involved. Treats partners fairly.

- Establishes collaborative partnerships to enhance organizational capacity to reach mission goals.

- Identifies barriers to effective communication and identifies ways to overcome them.

- Demonstrates alertness to opportunities to maximize resources, improve services, and avoid unnecessary duplication through collaborative and partnership efforts.

- Meets independently with external stakeholders and influential parties to answer questions about the organization's work policies.

- Minimizes stove-piping and other sources of disruptive competition among work groups.

Behavioral Examples Targeted for Managers

Competency: **Political Savvy**

Definition: Identifies the internal and external politics impacting the work of the organization. Perceives organizational and political reality and acts accordingly.

Behavioral Examples for the Manager Role

- Balances individual unit interests with broader organizational realities to arrive at the best solution for all stakeholders and constituents.
- Builds and strengthens enduring bases of support.
- Involves key stakeholders and organization leaders in decision-making or problem-solving activities that may have political implications.
- Monitors political, economic, and social trends that may affect the internal structures of the organization.
- Recognizes the dynamics of ongoing power and political relationships within the organization.
- Recognizes the impact on stakeholders of alternate courses of action.
- Takes advantage of opportunities to build relations and political capital with industry, other organizations, or federal, state and local governments.
- Understands how the organization interacts with the external world; relations with the public, stakeholders, media, Congress, and special interest groups and uses this knowledge in achieving results.
- Understands the forces shaping views and actions of clients, customers, or competitors.
- Understands when the decks is stacked against your position or interests; knows when to walk away.

Behavioral Examples Targeted for Managers

Competency: **Strategic Thinking**

Definition: Formulates objectives and priorities, and implements plans consistent with the long-term interests of the organization in a global environment. Capitalizes on opportunities and manages risks.

Behavioral Examples for the Manager Role

- Builds and uses an adequate knowledge base and knowledge management system to recognize success factors, provide feedback, and alert to change and opportunity.
- Contributes to a strategic thinking and planning process by monitoring and analyzing the impact of national and international policies, and social, economic, and political trends.
- Develops and aligns strategies of the unit to accomplish the goals of the organization.
- Involves key stakeholders and employees in the strategic planning process for an organizational unit.
- Makes realistic assessments of resource requirements and priorities for organizational unit as input to strategic thinking.
- Plans for and invests in training and other developmental activities for self and others enhancing the abilities of the group to meet strategic goals.
- Plans the implementation and management of the organization's strategic plan.
- Broadly reaches out to other organizations, groups, and disciplines to solicit ideas and perspectives of others in order to generate the best solutions.

Behavioral Examples Targeted for Managers

Competency: **Technology Management**

Definition: Keeps up to date on technological developments. Makes effective use of technology to achieve results. Ensures access to and security of technology systems.

Behavioral Examples for the Manager Role

- Employs a knowledge management system that supports decision making with the right information available to the right people at the right time.
- Ensures business processes are reengineered to be consistent with opportunities presented by changing technology.
- Ensures recovery plans and backup systems are in place for mission-critical records.
- Keeps a long-range and systems view of how work, services, and programs can be enhanced through technology.
- Links IT investment decisions to strategic objectives and business plans.
- Promotes development of IT programs and support systems that better ensure seamless delivery of services and ease of use.
- Strategically and systematically plans for IT training/education across the organization, and monitors the effectiveness of this training.
- Tracks underperforming projects and makes corrective actions.
- Keeps abreast of technological developments impacting own discipline and world of work with an eye toward adopting appropriate technology.

Behavioral Examples for Managers

Competency: **Accountability**

Definition: Holds self and others accountable for measurable high-quality, timely, and cost-effective results. Determines objectives, sets priorities, and delegates work. Accepts responsibility for mistakes. Complies with established control systems and rules.

Behavioral Examples for the Manager Role

- Develops and implements a system to ensure measurement of program outcomes and reporting on results.
- Develops mechanisms to allow customers and employees to provide regular feedback.
- Evaluates organizational plans and budgets in accordance with organizational policies and procedures and applicable laws & regulations.
- Evaluates program performance and project accomplishments to assess overall program effectiveness and efficiency.
- Identifies performance measures of organizational results and systems to affect accountability.
- Implements human resource strategies resulting in the hiring and development of high-quality public servants whose skills match the changing needs of the organization.
- Takes holistic view of organization's mission, looking beyond institutional boundaries.
- Takes initiative to seek out partnerships and other cross-cutting ways of work that might result in greater effectiveness or efficiency.
- Reviews employee churn data to find units with low employee engagement in order to increase engagement and reduce employee turnover.

Behavioral Examples for Managers

Competency: **Cross-Cultural Interactions**

Definition: Interacts with people of other cultures with ease. Communicates and performs over distance, culture, and time differences. Understands the impact of culture on management strategy and style.

Behavioral Examples for the Manager Role

- Understands the conditions in which culture can influence behaviours and that it is now becoming even more important as factors such as digitalisation and globalization lead to even greater cross-cultural interactions.

- Reads books about diverse cultures in order to understand them better.

- Reaches out to new, nontraditional groups to educate them about the work of the organization.

- Is open to the contributions of diverse colleagues, employees, and stakeholders; seeks and acknowledges their input.

- Creates an informal cross-cultural advisor team to help share knowledge about different cultures within the group to increase the pool of knowledge about these cultures.

- Interacts with people from different backgrounds with an attitude of respect and acceptance, seeking to build relationships on shared values, vision, and mission.

- Seeks to mentor a diverse group of people, seeking to share experience and counsel and wisdom with people across cultures.

Behavioral Examples for Managers

Competency: **Conflict Management**

Definition: Encourages creative tension and differences of opinions. Anticipates and takes steps to prevent counterproductive confrontations. Manages and resolves conflicts and disagreements in a constructive manner.

Behavioral Examples for the Manager Role

- Ensures first-level supervisors have the authority to resolve conflicts early without fear of negative impact on them or their careers.

- Holds self and others accountable for the maintenance of an organizational culture whose practices embody fairness, inclusiveness, respect, and civility.

- Demonstrates knowledge of group and organization dynamics as well as strategies, techniques, and resources that minimize conflict within them.

- Provides organizational support and resources, (e.g., programs and training for employees) to help them manage and resolve conflict in a positive and constructive manner.

- Provides support to supervisors in resolving grievances and EEO complaints that reach management level.

- Strategically plans to advance seamless and interdepartmental approaches to services and products.

- Positively uses conflict to help the organization evolve.

Competency: **Continual Learning**

Definition: Assesses and recognizes own strengths and weaknesses. Pursues self-development.

Behavioral Examples for the Manager Role

- Clearly define training goals and expectations, and link these to organizational objectives, mission, and goals.

- Design and implement knowledge management systems which span the breadth of your span of control allowing you real-time access to decision-making data.

- Model continuous self-development.

- Strategically plan to meet changing organizational needs in skills and knowledge.

- Regularly solicit employees' ideas on key issues, as a built-in part of the planning and evaluation processes.

- Understand and apply knowledge and techniques of organizational development to build the organization's capacity to learn, improve, anticipate and meet new challenges.

Behavioral Examples for Managers

Competency: **Customer Service**

Definition: Anticipates and meets the needs of both internal and external customers. Delivers high-quality products and services. Demonstrates commitment to continuous improvement.

Behavioral Examples for the Manager Role

- Ensures first-line supervisors effectively address episodes of poor customer service.

- Identifies systems barriers to providing good customer service.

- Identifies ways to provide access to the organization's services for all groups.

- Demonstrates accessibility to all customers, including staff.

- Promotes an active and dynamic customer focus throughout the organization, through performance expectations and the use of processes that are participative, interactive, and proactive.

- Rewards creativity in the pursuit of excellent customer service.

- Understands how various services are linked and uses partnering to achieve the greatest benefit to the customer.

- Uses customer feedback data to continuously plan, provide, and improve products and services.

Behavioral Examples for Managers

Competency: **Decisiveness**

Definition: Makes effective and timely decisions, even when data are limited or solutions produce unpleasant consequences. Perceives the impact and implications of decisions.

Behavioral Examples for the Manager Role

- Anticipates need for action, consequences of acting (or not acting), potential problems, or opportunities.
- Assumes responsibility for risks taken and actions pursued throughout the organization consistent with organization policies and procedures.
- Demonstrates skill in formulating objectives and strategies under pressure and for complex situations.
- Empowers others to take risks, supports them when things are difficult, and encourages them to learn from setbacks and failures.
- Ensures policies and procedures are in place encouraging decision making and action orientation at the appropriate levels.
- Examines/considers political, financial, social, and industry and international implications and impacts before reaching final decisions.
- Knows how to organize for effective decisions.
- Makes sound, timely decisions for an organization about staff, equipment, facilities, or funds.
- Seeks to balance short-term gains and long-term needs of the organization when making decisions.
- Uses a structured approach to decision making with an articulable model to help bring rigor to the decision making process.

Behavioral Examples for Managers

Competency: **Developing Others**

Definition: Develops the ability of others to perform and contribute to the organization by providing ongoing feedback and by providing opportunities to learn through formal and informal methods.

Behavioral Examples for the Manager Role

- Defines training goals and expectations for the organization, linking individual development to organization strategic objectives, mission, and goals.
- Consults with supervisors when issues concerning fair and adequate distribution of development activities arise.
- Ensures direct reports have appropriate training to perform their duties in meeting program goals.
- Ensures training and development plans meet needed competencies and measures the results.
- Helps the members of the organization learn from customers and stakeholders and translate that learning into improved performance.
- Provides direct reports with ongoing feedback on areas of strength and needed development.
- Uses a systematic process and the advice of experts to analyze competency gaps, plan appropriate developmental interventions, collect relevant performance data, and evaluate the results of the interventions.
- Uses organization and program goals to determine focus of development activities for upcoming fiscal year.

Behavioral Examples for Managers

Competency: **Entrepreneurship**

Definition: Positions the organization for future success by identifying new opportunities. Builds the organization by developing or improving products or services. Takes calculated risks to accomplish organizational objectives.

Behavioral Examples for the Manager Role

- Resolves resource limitations using innovative approaches.

- Anticipates and resolves logistical and resource challenges to new products, services, processes, or systems.

- Changes standard operating procedures, occupational patterns, and traditional power structures as necessary to implement improvements.

- Demonstrates knowledge of innovative approaches to government and business to look for ways to streamline expensive, time-consuming processes.

- Promotes a culture of innovation and a willingness to try new things without fear of reprisal.

- Recognizes and accepts risk of failure in suggesting and developing innovation in products or service delivery.

- Takes initiative leading to different markets or new clients/customers for the organization.

- Uses others' knowledge to find potential supporters of innovation and works proactively to get them on board.

Behavioral Examples for Managers

Competency: **External Awareness**

Definition: Understands and keeps up to date on local, national, and international policies and trends that affect the organization and shape stakeholders' views. Aware of the organization's impact on the external environment.

Behavioral Examples for the Manager Role

- Cultivates a global mindset; regularly scans a wide variety of information sources to identify political, social, economic trends that impacts the organization's mission.

- Ensures correspondence, reports, and policy documents are consistent with policies and priorities, and are sensitive to stakeholder views.

- Demonstrates awareness of current trends, opportunities, and threats to the organization's mission.

- Uses political savvy in addressing, informing, and negotiating buy-in from all key stakeholders.

- Promotes analysis of appropriate data (e.g., technology forecasting, decision analysis, statistical models) to understand the impact of external activities on organizational actions, and develops strategies.

- Understands and manages relationships with adversarial stakeholders.

- Uses understanding of systemic structures to anticipate and respond to external change.

Behavioral Examples for Managers

Competency: **Flexibility**

Definition: Demonstrates openness to change and new information. Rapidly adapts to new information, changing conditions, or unexpected obstacles.

Behavioral Examples for the Manager Role

- Demonstrates an ability to assess a crisis situation, manage the overwhelming amounts of information a crisis generates, marshal resources, and organize for effective decisions.

- Adjusts and uses concepts, methods, and approaches that have been successfully used by others.

- Identifies key stakeholders, sponsors, and potential advocates and detractors, and develops appropriate strategies for each group.

- Demonstrates openness to new ideas and approaches that improve service and reduce costs in an organizational unit.

- Generates multiple solutions to problems and approaches to improvement, then uses modeling techniques, risk analysis, and cost-benefit analysis to assess their strategic and tactical impact.

- Demonstrates alertness to emerging opportunities and can maneuver the organization to take advantage of them.

- Maintains organization's productivity, quality, and morale during changes in one or more of the following:

deadlines; requirements/specifications; budget/staff
resources; technology; organizational structure;
management philosophy; leadership; legal or policy
requirements; workplace environment or conditions;
telecommuting; and flexible work schedules.

- Scans the organization's political, social, economic,
  environmental, and technological environments for new
  information and to pick up shifts in relationships,
  priorities, and needs.

Behavioral Examples for Managers

Competency: **Human Capital Management**

Definition: Builds and manages workforce based on organizational goals, budget considerations, and staffing needs. Ensures employees are appropriately recruited, selected, appraised, and rewarded. Takes action to address performance problems. Manage a multi-sector workforce and a variety of work situations.

Behavioral Examples for the Manager Role

- Actively involves labor partners in formulating new human resource practices.

- Analyzes and strategically plans for a workforce with skills and competencies that meet current, emerging, and future challenges.

- Balances technical competence with leadership competencies when selecting and developing supervisory personnel.

- Encourages supervisors to recognize and reward people and teams based on effective performance.

- Plans for and manages an increasingly diverse, multi-sector, blended workforce employed in a wide variety of traditional and nontraditional employment arrangements.

- Uses performance goals and measures to ensure the management of human resources contributes to the accomplishment of the organization's mission.

Behavioral Examples for Managers

Competency: **Influencing and Negotiating**

Definition: Persuades others. Builds consensus through give and take. Gains cooperation from others to obtain information and accomplish goals.

Behavioral Examples for the Manager Role

- Effectively shapes the debate and influences how an issue and potential solutions are perceived by others.
- Communicates evolving conditions upward and makes their implications for the health of the organization clear.
- Develops effective business cases for change and new initiatives.
- Adapts arguments and presentations to the specific interest level of the audience.
- Understands and communicates internal and external factors and interdependencies, including global considerations having an impact on policy setting and the organization's work.
- Recognizes the needs and perceptions of key stakeholders and is able to effectively balance and weigh competing interests.
- Understands and uses active listening, effective verbal communication, personal integrity, flexibility, emotional control, analysis and evaluation skills in negotiation situations.
- Uses intercultural knowledge and skill to increase effectiveness as a representative in negotiations and discussions with other organizations.

Behavioral Examples for Managers

Competency: **Integrity and Honesty**

Definition: Behaves in an honest, fair, and ethical manner. Shows consistency in words and actions. Creates a culture that fosters high ethical standards.

Behavioral Examples for the Manager Role

- Assures effective systems are in place to communicate regulations, programs, and guidelines about ethics.
- Creates a climate supporting integrity and honesty in the organization, through personal example and through processes and procedures that reward and encourage ethical behavior.
- Fairly distributes opportunities and benefits across the entire organization.
- Keeps the confidence of performance discussions, mentoring, and personal issues raised by the employee.
- Protects the privacy of employees, customers, and other members of the public.
- Opposes what is wrong and has the fortitude to support ethical actions that may negatively impact certain stakeholders of the organization.
- Supports supervisors in taking action to assure regulations adherence.
- Understands diversity and inclusiveness—not merely as democratic mandates, but as tremendous sources of strength and acts accordingly in hiring, development, group organization, and decision making.
- Understands the legal and ethical frameworks does not take action against it, even when such a course might seem to offer some benefit.

Behavioral Examples for Managers

Competency: **Interpersonal Skill**

Definition: Treats others with courtesy, sensitivity, and respect. Considers and appropriately responds to the needs and feelings of different people in different situations.

Behavioral Examples for the Manager Role

- Builds better communications and cooperation between levels and across the organization's divisions and units.

- Coaches, teaches, counsels, and motivates employees toward greater mutual respect and understanding.

- Confronts performance problems in a way that maintains a positive relationship.

- Ensures all partners are fairly and ethically treated.

- Exhibits tact, restraint, and professionalism in difficult situations dealing with topics of concern to the organization.

- Involves people in the decisions that affect them such as with work schedules, assignments, and rewards.

- Demonstrates openness and approachability, is decisive without being arrogant or abrupt when dealing with sensitive and complex issues.

- Maintains effective relations with external groups affected by the organization's policies and program activities.

Behavioral Examples for Managers

Competency: **Leveraging Diversity**

Definition: Fosters an inclusive workplace where diversity and individual differences are valued and leveraged to achieve the vision and mission of the organization.

Behavioral Examples for the Manager Role

- Assures systems are in place to have reasonable accommodations for individual differences to ensure the full potential of all employees.

- Develops and implements plans for assessing and dealing with concerns and needs of persons with disabilities to include work equipment, building modification (such as bathroom accessibility), and interpreters.

- Possesses a global perspective and is able to work and coordinate work across cultural and national differences.

- Makes managing workforce diversity a performance criterion for supervisors.

- Manages succession planning in a way that produces a diverse, prepared leader pool.

- Sets a personal example of civility and inclusiveness.

- Sets a personal example of soliciting and considering diverse viewpoints and ideas.

Behavioral Examples for Managers

Competency: **Oral Communication**

Definition: Makes clear and convincing oral presentations. Listens effectively; clarifies information as needed. Facilitates open communication.

Behavioral Examples for the Manager Role

- Demonstrates an ability to effectively shape the debate and influence how an issue and potential solutions are perceived by others.

- Communicates with customers, employees, and other key stakeholders with openness and transparency.

- Conducts debriefing of stressful situations as needed.

- Ensures others understand the power of open communication to enhance workplace relationships and that they have the communication skills to be effective members of a learning organization.

- Identifies barriers to effective communication and identifies ways to overcome them.

- Models assertive communication and positive attitudes even in extremely challenging situations.

- Plans and implements a crisis communications strategy that can support quick and flexible organizational responses to unforeseen, new, and complex situations.

- Uses fact, reason, and persuasion to bring others in line with the vision, rather than skewed arguments representing an unfair presentation of the issue.

Behavioral Examples for Managers

Competency: **Problem Solving**

Definition: Identifies and analyzes problems. Weighs information relevance and accuracy. Generates and evaluates alternative solutions. Makes recommendations.

Behavioral Examples for the Manager Role

- Determines the best way to implement new policies and programs by engaging key players in identifying the root causes of problems, possible roadblocks, and alternative solutions.
- Assists others in understanding and handling the forces and opportunities requiring changes of thought and approach.
- Identifies gaps in knowledge and modifies data gathering and analysis processes to fill those gaps.
- Involves appropriate clients, stakeholders, and staff in problem solving.
- Practices and teaches decision-making tools proven to help distinguish among choices in ethical dilemmas and in weighing risk.
- Recognizes the impact on constituencies of alternate courses of action. Understands the drawbacks that may be incurred with short-term, quick fixes.
- Understands what information is statistically meaningful.
- Works closely with cooperators to provide seamless resolutions from a customer's point of view.
- Focuses on removing barriers for those working within own area of responsibility, forcefully removing barriers fully within own area of responsibility and working with partners when the barrier is shared.

Behavioral Examples for Managers

Competency: **Resilience**

Definition: Effectively deals with pressure. Remains optimistic and persistent, even under adversity. Quickly recovers from setbacksHere

Behavioral Examples for the Manager Role

- Demonstrates the ability to assess a crisis situation, manage overwhelming amounts of information that crisis generates; organize for effective decisions.
- Designs and implements key strategic processes and programs allowing the organization to remain productive during times of crisis, other uncertainty, rapid change, and other common stress-producing conditions.
- Encourages use of existing policies and programs that help employees balance work, personal life, and wellness.
- Provides structure and information helping employees and organizational units understand how to react positively to new demands and circumstances, and how to employ existing resources to fulfill new mandates.
- Puts systems in place ensuring a safe, secure, and healthy workplace.
- Routinely assesses the quality of the workplace environment and culture.
- Translates organizational priorities and rebalances resources appropriately.
- Understands the organization from a systems perspective to minimize surprises and maximize ability to accurately forecast direction and needs.
- Understands when demands exceed the capacity of the organization to respond, and, when it is necessary, refuses unreasonable demands.

Behavioral Examples for Managers

Competency: **Team Building**

Definition: Inspires and fosters team commitment, spirit, pride, and trust. Facilitates cooperation and motivates team members to accomplish group goals.

Behavioral Examples for the Manager Role

- Uses membership on management level teams to further organizational goals.

- Communicates importance of team projects and gives high organizational visibility to successful projects.

- Creates innovative performance management and reward systems reinforcing team work.

- Encourages and supports first-line supervisors' recognition/rewards to team members.

- Ensures teams are given substantive issues with real potential impact on which to work.

- Works with project team coordinator to ensure teams have necessary resources and are working synergistically in support of overarching organizational goals.

- Spearheads the use of cross-functional teams to increase organizational effectiveness.

- Uses teaming to address complex problems that both affect and require attention from a number of individuals and groups. Maximizes involvement of relevant personnel and subject experts across and outside of the organization.

Behavioral Examples for Managers

Competency: **Technical Credibility**

Definition: Understands and appropriately applies principles, procedures, requirements, regulations, and policies related to specialized expertise.

Behavioral Examples for the Manager Role

- Nurtures innovations recognized as best practices.

- Invests in hiring and essential resources to support extension of organizational expertise.

- Anticipates and builds technical capacity needed for the future.

- Encourages first-line supervisors to seek information about new procedures, requirements, regulations, and policies, and to become an expert on matters relating to innovative solutions.

- Seeks input from others when in-depth subject matter expertise outside of own area is required.

- Encourages supervisors to see that supervisory effectiveness is a needed focus in their development of technical credibility.

Behavioral Examples for Managers

Competency: **Vision**

Definition: Takes a long-term view and builds a shared vision with others. Acts as a catalyst for organizational change. Influences others to translate vision into action.

Behavioral Examples for the Manager Role

- Transforms visionary goals into practical tactics, strategic plans, and achievable actions.

- Anticipates, recognizes, and helps to remedy individual or collective barriers to the implementation of change.

- Builds support and commitment across the full range of stakeholders.

- Clearly communicates the message or vision in terms of tangible goals to everyone affected, and actively involves them in the change process.

- Develops strategies to attract, motivate, and retain superior employees with the flexible skills and abilities necessary to meet complex challenges and change.

- Ensures change message is heard. Takes efforts to deliver the message or vision for change to everyone affected.

- Helps staff members understand how their function or unit relates to and complements the overall organizational vision and mission.

- Recognizes and communicates contributions and progress toward visionary goals.

Behavioral Examples for Managers

Competency: **Written Communication**

Definition: Writes in a clear, concise, organized, and convincing manner for the intended audience.

Behavioral Examples for the Manager Role

- Creates a written voice that is personal, visible, and recognizable and that inspires trust and commitment among employees and stakeholders.

- Creates widespread ownership and commitment to the organization's policies, goals, and strategies by keeping stakeholders and employees informed.

- Edits to avoid stereotypes, region-specific metaphors and images, and innuendoes.

- Writes convincingly for continued stakeholder support in the face of challenges to policy or strategy.

- Avoids humor in written documents with an international audience, as humor is culture specific.

- Demonstrates awareness of the background knowledge of the recipients of a written communication.

Chapter 7:
Leadership Development for Executives

Primary focus:
Leading and Managing the Organization

Core Competencies:
- Entrepreneurship
- External Awareness
- Vision

Leadership Role Continuum
All Employees --> Team Leader --> Supervisor --> Manager --> **Executive**

Are you in an executive role or want to be in an executive role? The following pages spell out the leadership competencies and the behavioral examples for the role of team leader.

Follow the process as outlined in Chapter 2:

1. Identify your goal
2. Assess proficiency
3. Identify learning experiences
4. Create your development plan
5. Complete learning experiences
6. Assess progress
7. Repeat

As you work through your development plan, review the behavioral examples on the following pages. These examples should provide you with a fairly comprehensive view of what the leadership competencies look like for the role of executive.

Behavioral Examples Targeted for Executives

Competency: **Entrepreneurship**

Definition: Positions the organization for future success by identifying new opportunities; builds the organization by developing or improving products or services. Takes calculated risks to accomplish organizational objectives.

Behavioral Examples for the Executive Role

- Champions improvement and innovation in government; strategically works to move beyond individual acts of innovation to the innovative organization.

- Develops new options for customer services delivery.

- Enhances the organization's ability (and the ability of larger stakeholder coalitions) to effectively and efficiently respond to interrelated issues.

- Involves the private or voluntary sector to achieve public purposes, including competitions, partnerships, and use of voluntary services.

- Demonstrates strategic and forward thinking, continually reviewing, developing, and improving systems.

- Understands the regulatory environment; knows and can use the process by which obsolete regulations and laws can be changed.

- Works effectively in the political environment to combat inadequate funding, political opposition, and legal and regulatory restraints unnecessarily impeding progress toward service goals.

- Gains political support; builds effective change alliances.

Behavioral Examples Targeted for Executives

Competency: **External Awareness**

Definition: Understands and keeps up to date on local, national, and international policies and trends that affect the organization and shape stakeholders' views. Aware of the organization's impact on the external environment.

Behavioral Examples for the Executive Role

- Demonstrates an understanding of the national policy-making and implementation processes.
- Explains and defends the organization's policies and operations to the external world in order to gain the support needed to assure program success.
- Possesses a global breadth of perspective and demonstrates an ability to work and coordinate work cross-culturally, nationally, internationally, and globally.
- Demonstrates an awareness of current trends, opportunities, and threats to the organization's mission.
- Makes organizational boundaries permeable; encourages communities of practice.
- Recognizes the possible impact of international events and global issues of environment and economy on U.S. society, the government, and the organization.
- Influences the decision-making processes to ensure policies, programs, and other developments are informed, customer driven, and considered within the broad political framework.
- When representing the organization, demonstrates sensitivity to the political, social, and cultural nuances of difficult issues.

Behavioral Examples Targeted for Executives

Competency: **Vision**

Definition: Takes a long-term view and builds a shared vision with others. Acts as a catalyst for organizational change. Influences others to translate vision into action

Behavioral Examples for the Executive Role

- Breaks down organizational barriers to help the organization achieve its vision and mission.

- Creates a vision of administrative capacity across agencies, with NGOs, and international organizations to effectively address problems in a sustained and articulated rather than stove-piped fashion.

- Demonstrates commitment to organization's vision and mission.

- Develops infrastructure, plans, and processes for translating vision into action.

- Participates in knowledge and policy networks and ensures Agency participation in such networks.

- Provides a clear vision of where the organization is headed and leads the organization through necessary changes.

- Shares the "big picture" with staff.

- Steers the organization toward its higher service purpose through the development, articulation, and implementation of organizational vision.

Behavioral Examples for Executives

Competency: **Accountability**

Definition: Holds self and others accountable for measurable high-quality, timely, and cost-effective results. Determines objectives, sets priorities, and delegates work. Accepts responsibility for mistakes. Complies with established control systems and rules.

Behavioral Examples for the Executive Role

- Develops a framework for defining and measuring program outcomes and reporting results across the enterprise.

- Ensures effectiveness of accountability controls within the organization to include management reviews, program evaluations, financial statements audits.

- Ensures all Managers, Supervisors, and employees are trained to understand management control responsibilities.

- Ensures program, financial, and performance measures are integrated to assess and achieve strategic outcomes.

- Evaluates both program and procedures to determine program improvement or elimination.

- Oversees the establishment, development, monitoring, and maintenance of an organization-wide performance management system.

- Broadly works with stakeholders to create a shared vision, balancing and reconciling various interests.

Behavioral Examples for Executives

Competency: **Conflict Management**

Definition: Encourages creative tension and differences of opinions. Anticipates and takes steps to prevent counterproductive confrontations. Manages and resolves conflicts and disagreements in a constructive manner.

Behavioral Examples for the Executive Role

- Actively seeks out involvement and input from key stakeholders outside the Agency on potentially difficult and contentious issues before deciding on a course of action.

- Actively shapes the organizational climate by setting, sustaining, exemplifying, and celebrating an inclusive and civil environment.

- Holds managers accountable for preventing and resolving conflict at the earliest stage.

- Encourages creative conflict leading to better ideas, systems, processes, and relationships.

- Promotes shared authority and power to prevent and resolve conflict.

- Uses the creative energy that comes from tensions between seemingly opposing forces, ideas, and directions.

- Uses sound, balanced judgment in resolving complaints from a high-level customer or stakeholder.

Behavioral Examples for Executives

Competency: **Continual Learning**

Definition: Assesses and recognizes own strengths and weaknesses. Pursues self-development.

Behavioral Examples for the Executive Role

- Assesses and demonstrates how training and development efforts contribute to improved performance and results.

- Communicates throughout the organization the need to understand others' viewpoints, agendas, values, constraints, and behaviors, and demonstrates a willingness to take others' ideas into consideration.

- Creates a climate where continuous learning and self-development are valued.

- Develops a strategic approach establishing priorities in training and development to achieve organizational results.

- Ensures managers and supervisors have been properly trained to coach, evaluate, and conduct employee career discussions.

- Incorporates employees' development goals into the organization's planning process.

- Promotes benchmarking and other techniques that help the organization build upon best practices.

- Provides consistent support and appropriate funding for training and development efforts.

Behavioral Examples for Executives

Competency: **Creativity and Innovation**

Definition: Develops new insights into situations. Questions conventional approaches. Encourages new ideas and innovations. Designs and implements new or cutting- edge programs and/or processes.

Behavioral Examples for the Executive Role

- Breaks down barriers, stereotypes, and impediments to achieving breakthrough results and quality service.

- Builds an organization that attracts, motivates, and retains superior employees who demonstrate creativity and innovation.

- Encourages demonstration projects, pilots, and other experimental approaches.

- Infuses big-picture or systems thinking throughout the organization in developing strategic plans.

- Engages in government-wide improvement initiatives.

- Demonstrates strategic and forward thinking, continually reviewing, developing, and improving systems.

- Looks beyond current reality to prepare organization for alternative futures.

- Serves as champion for new ideas and approaches and articulates linkage between new behaviors and organizational success.

Behavioral Examples for Executives

Competency: **Cross-Cultural Interactions**

Definition: Interacts with people of other cultures with ease. Communicates and performs over distance, culture, and time differences. Understands the impact of culture on management strategy and style.

Behavioral Examples for the Executive Role

- Reads books about diverse cultures in order to understand them better.

- Reaches out to new, nontraditional groups to educate them about the work of the organization.

- Is open to the contributions of diverse colleagues, employees, and stakeholders; seeks and acknowledges their input.

- Ensures that formal stakeholder groups, such as boards and committees, are representative of the diversity of the the stakeholder group.

- Receives and considers counsel from a diverse set of counselors, advisors, and mentors.

- Creates an informal cross-cultural advisor team to help share knowledge about different cultures within the group to increase the pool of knowledge about these cultures.

Competency: **Customer Service**

Definition: Anticipates and meets the needs of both internal and external customers. Delivers high-quality products and services. Demonstrates commitment to continuous improvement.

Behavioral Examples for the Executive Role

- Communicates the value of continuous customer feedback and input by serving as an example to all employees.

- Establishes a customer-oriented culture and promotes hiring people who fit that culture and performance expectation.

- Establishes a customer-focused business strategy that includes customer feedback and needs in strategic plans and results in measurable improvements in customer satisfaction.

- Identifies ways to provide access to the organization's services for all groups.

- Integrates marketing into overall business planning.

- Demonstrates the ability to be politically adroit in addressing, informing, and negotiating buy-in from all key stakeholders.

- Shares resources across the organization in order to effectively and efficiently serve customers.

- Takes full account of appropriate issues, their interrelationships and implications for service and business development.

Behavioral Examples for Executives

Competency: **Decisiveness**

Definition: Makes effective and timely decisions, even when data are limited or solutions produce unpleasant consequences. Perceives the impact and implications of decisions.

Behavioral Examples for the Executive Role

- Anticipates need for action and the potential problems or opportunities of acting, or not acting.

- Commits the organization to a course of action when negotiating with external stakeholders.

- Ensures policies and procedures are in place encouraging decision making and action at the appropriate levels.

- Establishes strategic communications, plans, and alternatives for use in crisis situations.

- Improvises within the law and regulatory intent to achieve the organization's mission.

- Makes sound, timely, and often courageous decisions.

- Quickly condenses research and evidence into realistic implementation and strategy.

- Takes reasoned (educated and informed) risks to achieve organizational goals.

- Uses a decision making model that includes actively addressing enterprise risk.

Behavioral Examples for Executives

Competency: **Developing Others**

Definition: Develops the ability of others to perform and contribute to the organization by providing ongoing feedback and by providing opportunities to learn through formal and informal methods

Behavioral Examples for the Executive Role

- Communicates the principle of life-long learning and provides opportunities for continuous development.
- Develops employee development strategy and training focus in accordance with organizational direction and program goals.
- Establishes policy for managers and supervisors on use of self-assessments, assessments by others, and 360° assessments to determine their annual development goals.
- Identifies mission-critical knowledge, skills, and competencies for all levels and establishes objectives and strategies for achieving them.
- Promotes interagency, cross-governmental, private sector, and international developmental efforts as appropriate.
- Provides direct reports with ongoing feedback on areas of strength and needed development.
- Provides shadowing and detail assignments for potential executives.
- Reviews training goals and processes in light of strategic and tactical changes.

Behavioral Examples for Executives

Competency: **Financial Management**

Definition: Understands the organization's financial processes. Prepares, justifies, and administers the program budget. Oversees procurement and contracting to achieve desired results. Monitors expenditures and uses cost-benefit thinking to set priorities.

Behavioral Examples for the Executive Role

- Demonstrates knowledge of budget and funding process.

- Ensures appropriate administrative control of funds.

- Ensures people with the requisite knowledge and skills are in place to advise and participate in budget planning, evaluation, and financial systems.

- Maintains citizen confidence in the effectiveness and efficiency of Federal work.

- Plans strategic budgets to close the gap between the current situation and the organization's longer-term goals.

- Provides testimony or support to head of organization during Congressional/legislative testimony or meetings of other high-level organizations resulting in positive action.

- Applies marketing principles and tools as appropriate to increase awareness and encourage the use of products and services.

- Effectively leverages resources across relevant programs and service.

Behavioral Examples for Executives

Competency: **Flexibility**

Definition: Demonstrates openness to change and new information. Rapidly adapts to new information, changing conditions, or unexpected obstacles.

Behavioral Examples for the Executive Role

- Demonstrates an ability to assess a crisis situation, manage overwhelming amounts of information that crises generates, marshal resources, and organize for effective decisions.
- Communicates a vision of change that broadly appeals to the long-term interests of critical stakeholders.
- Identifies key stakeholders, sponsors, potential advocates, and detractors and develops appropriate strategies for each group.
- Forms contingency plans to overcome potential obstacles, and to take advantage of unforeseeable opportunities.
- Generates multiple solutions to problems and approaches to improvement, then uses modeling techniques, risk analysis, and cost-benefit analysis to assess their strategic and tactical impact.
- Establishes key strategic planning and evaluation processes enabling the organization to remain responsive to changing circumstances, priorities, and resources.
- Uses ethical as well as strategic considerations when deciding when to be flexible and when to remain firmly on course.
- Responds to changing priorities and resources with optimism, encouraging staff to respond positively and proactively.
- Stays abreast of and educates staff about changing national and international conditions affecting agricultural programs, policies, and strategies.

Behavioral Examples for Executives

Competency: **Human Capital Management**

Definition: Builds and manages workforce based on organizational goals, budget considerations, and staffing needs. Ensures employees are appropriately recruited, selected, appraised, and rewarded; takes action to address performance problems. Manages a multi-sector workforce and a variety of work situations.

Behavioral Examples for the Executive Role

- Bases human capital plans and programs on timely, well-researched, and well-analyzed trends and data.
- Creates a workforce planning and analysis process to identify strategic human resource needs of the organization and develop strategies to meet the long-term needs of the organization.
- Ensures enterprise-wide accountability for the effective management of its people resources.
- Ensures employee rewards and recognition programs are reliably linked to performance that contributes to achievement of the enterprise organization's goals.
- Integrates human capital management into supervisor, manager, and executive performance expectations and holds them accountable for the good and efficient management of the organization's people resources.
- Positions the enterprise organization to address current challenges and meet emerging demands through a strategic and integrated approach to human capital management.
- Serves as an advocate for organizational and public policies that contribute to attracting and retaining top people including family-friendly programs, flexible work schedules, and alternate worksite locations.
- Systematically establishes plans and programs to acquire, develop, and manage strong leadership, managerial, and supervisory cadres.

Behavioral Examples for Executives

Competency: **Influencing and Negotiating**

Definition: Persuades others. Builds consensus through give and take. Gains cooperation from others to obtain information and accomplish goals.

Behavioral Examples for the Executive Role

- Builds, maintains, and impacts large internal and external virtual networks to build collaborative power and to achieve results.
- Commits resources appropriate to the task to resolve issues (e.g., employs outside facilitators to reach agreement).
- Communicates a clear and compelling vision that provides employees with a sense of direction and which can solicit broad support from key stakeholders.
- Consistently uses effective persuasion to gain consensus with others when representing the organization and its policies on intra- or inter-organizations and with employee associations or unions in reaching strategic goals.
- Establishes an overall environment influencing individuals and groups toward achieving the organization's goals.
- Inspires others to act at the highest level of honesty and integrity, and holds them accountable to it.
- Uses persuasion to gain consensus with other agencies, corporations, or national unions.
- Uses intercultural knowledge and skill to increase effectiveness in negotiations and discussion with officials of foreign governments.

Behavioral Examples for Executives

Competency: **Integrity and Honesty**

Definition: Behaves in an honest, fair, and ethical manner. Shows consistency in words and actions. Creates a culture that fosters high ethical standards.

Behavioral Examples for the Executive Role

- Acts with courage and consistency with espoused values, even when it might be unpopular, or personally inconvenient to do so.

- Creates an organizational culture that fosters high ethical standards, service, and honor.

- Ensures policies and programs for preventing waste, fraud, abuse, and mismanagement are in place and enforced.

- Ensures the organization has the information to act using the full breadth of allowance, yet transgressing neither against the law itself nor against public perception of what is right.

- Demonstrates responsiveness to elected leaders and faithfulness to Constitutional values and processes.

- Models behaviors, attitudes, and actions expected of all employees.

- Provides accurate, current, and understandable information to policy makers and citizens, exposing the implications of choice in an unbiased fashion.

- Serves as a role model of integrity, honesty, justice, respect, and civility.

Behavioral Examples for Executives

Competency: **Interpersonal Skills**

Definition: Treats others with courtesy, sensitivity, and respect. Considers appropriately responds to the needs and feelings of different people in different situations.

Behavioral Examples for the Executive Role

- Promptly corrects problems and without defensiveness.

- Seeks to understand the cultures, beliefs, values, biases, preferences, feelings, and other drivers of behavior—both conscious and unconscious—in oneself and others.

- Demonstrate discretion and tact when correcting or questioning another's idea or action.

- Seeks accurate information, avoids jumping to conclusions or passing on questionable information.

- Seeks feedback from others to avoid blind spots that can cause misunderstandings.

- Shows respect for the values and ideas of others, even while not agreeing with them.

- Works effectively with many different people in a variety of settings (e.g., legislatures, professional associations) and gains their support.

- Appropriately and tactfully responds to the criticisms and concerns of external stakeholders.

Behavioral Examples for Executives

Competency: **Leveraging Diversity**

Definition: Fosters an inclusive workplace where diversity and individual differences are valued and leveraged to achieve the vision and mission of the organization.

Behavioral Examples for the Executive Role

- Develops short- and long-term strategies to create an inclusive, welcoming workplace designed to attract, acquire, and retain high-quality, diverse talent.

- Possesses a global breadth of perspective and is able to work and coordinate work cross-culturally, nationally, internationally, and globally.

- Promotes a broad-based diversity approach that significantly improves performance in the entire organization.

- Promotes diversity in succession planning to produce a diverse, prepared leader pool.

- Reaches out to other organizations, groups, and disciplines to solicit others' ideas and perspectives in order to generate the best solutions.

- Sets a personal example of soliciting and considering diverse viewpoints and ideas.

- Sets personal example of civility and inclusiveness.

- Holds management team accountable for ensuring fairness, equality, diversity, and reasonable accommodation are practiced within teams or work units.

Behavioral Examples for Executives

Competency: **Oral Communication**

Definition: Makes clear and convincing oral presentations. Listens effectively; clarifies information as needed. Facilitates open communication.

Behavioral Examples for the Executive Role

- Breaks down barriers to effective communication within and outside the organization.
- Communicates with customers, employees, and other key stakeholders with openness and transparency.
- Conducts credible and prudent briefing sessions for Congress or other national media.
- Creates a feedback-rich culture in which oral feedback is valued, sought out from a full range of stakeholders, broadly discussed, and acted upon.
- Promotes wide-spread ownership of the program vision, engendering the employee engagement needed to sustain the vision.
- Ensures others understand the power of open communication to enhance workplace relationships and ensures they have the oral communication skills to be effective members of a learning organization.
- Meets with external stakeholders and influential parties to answer questions about the organization's work policies, makes commitments, and negotiates agreements.
- Provides accurate, current, and understandable information to policy makers and citizens, explaining in an unbiased fashion where the organization is going and the implications of those decisions.

Behavioral Examples for Executives

Competency: **Partnering**

Definition: Develops networks and builds alliances. Collaborates across boundaries to build strategic relationships and achieve common goals.

Behavioral Examples for the Executive Role

- Possesses a global breadth of perspective and is able to work and coordinate work cross-culturally, nationally, internationally, and globally.
- Maintains a cooperative relationship with a wide range of constituencies in accomplishing complex organizational objectives.
- Networks with the full range of stakeholders, inside and outside the government, to identify and pursue high-potential service alliances.
- Participates in knowledge and policy networks and ensures Agency participation in such networks.
- Promotes coordination, cooperative agreements, and collaborative agreements among agencies.
- Broadly reaches out to other organizations, groups, and disciplines to solicit other ideas and perspectives in order to generate the best solutions.
- Supports staff in taking calculated risks in exploring new partnerships and other collaborative efforts.
- In public service, understands collaboration as a critical dimension of public service which is the key operational factor in achieving a citizen-focused, seamless government.

Behavioral Examples for Executives

Competency: **Political Savvy**

Definition: Identifies the internal and external politics that impact the work of the organization. Perceives organizational and political reality and acts accordingly.

Behavioral Examples for the Executive Role

- Analyzes current events and various environmental trends and posits possible changes of direction or processes.

- Balances interests of the organization with broader government purposes and realities to arrive at the best solution for public service.

- Ensures interests of the key stakeholders are addressed without compromising the integrity of the organization.

- Possesses a global breadth of perspective and is able to work and coordinate work cross-culturally, nationally, internationally, and globally.

- Possesses a strategic understanding of the issues and of how barriers to solutions might be addressed.

- Maps the organization's strategy, taking all internal and external environmental factors into account.

- Recognizes the possible impact of international events and global issues of environment and economy on U.S. society, the government, and the organization.

- Uses systems thinking to factor in the various organizations and stakeholder influences which will impact various organizational goal sets.

Behavioral Examples for Executives

Competency: **Problem Solving**

Definition: Identifies and analyzes problems. Weighs information relevance and accuracy. Generates and evaluates alternative solutions. Makes recommendations.

Behavioral Examples for the Executive Role

- Empowers others to act by relinquishing control—delegating authority and responsibility to others who may be closer to the problem communicates accountability.

- Ensures decisions are consistent with overall goals or organizational vision.

- Examines the complexities of and interrelationships among factors behind the problem, even when the problem seems simple and straightforward.

- Focuses on and resolves major problems based on an understanding of current and future conditions.

- Identifies opportunities for organizational success even in the context of uncertainty, problems, and threats.

- Models critical and creative thinking, problem solving; sees the possibilities in the situation.

- Broadly reaches out to other organizations, groups, and disciplines to solicit other ideas and perspectives in order to generate the best solutions.

- Supports managers and employees giving them freedom to solve problems on a timely basis.

Behavioral Examples for Executives

Competency: **Resilience**

Definition: Effectively deals with pressure. Remains optimistic and persistent, even under adversity. Quickly recovers from setbacks.

Behavioral Examples for the Executive Role

- Builds capacity in others to transform changes into challenges and opportunities.

- Conducts debriefings of stressful situations as needed.

- Designs and implements key strategic processes and programs that allow the organization to remain productive during times of crisis, other uncertainty, rapid change, and other common stress-producing conditions.

- Develops policies and provides programs helping employees balance work, personal life, and wellness.

- Maintains organizational effectiveness, service levels, stability, and morale of a major organization during times of great change.

- Models assertive communication and positive attitudes even in extremely challenging situations.

- Projects energy and optimism in the face of adversity influencing the entire organization.

- Understands the organization from a systems perspective to minimize surprises and maximize ability to accurately forecast direction and needs, moving the organization from reactive behavior to proactive initiatives.

Behavioral Examples for Executives

Competency: **Strategic Thinking**

Definition: Formulates objectives and priorities, and implements plans consistent with the long-term interests of the organization in a global environment. Capitalizes on opportunities and manages risks.

Behavioral Examples for the Executive Role

- Anticipates new, changed, or conflicting demands for programs and services, seeks information, and takes action.
- Develops alternative approaches and scenarios to accommodate different potential situations during planning.
- Develops strategies to integrate organizational strengths into the overall Agency mission.
- Ensures program, financial, and performance measures are integrated to achieve desired strategic outcomes.
- Involves employees and stakeholders in a strategic thinking and planning process to gain commitment and identify possible impediments.
- Maps the Agency strategy, taking all internal and external environmental factors into account.
- Puts systems in place to ensure the comprehensive review, reassessment, reprioritization, appropriate reengineering of what the organization does, how it does business, and who is involved in implementing its business.
- Reaches out to key stakeholders to ensure their perspectives are taken into account in all planning, and to enlist their support for the resulting plan.

Behavioral Examples for Executives

Competency: **Team Building**

Definition: Inspires and fosters team commitment, spirit, pride, and trust. Facilitates cooperation and motivates team members to accomplish group goals.

Behavioral Examples for the Executive Role

- Communicates importance of team projects and gives high organizational visibility to successful projects.

- Forms and tasks highly experienced teams to solve complex, high-profile problems involving overall organizational climate, mission, cross-cutting policy issues, customer, or other issues with major external focus.

- Implements the results of team efforts contributing to organization goals.

- Models importance of collaborative working through personal participation in high-level, interdisciplinary, cross-functional groups and teams that represent broad aspects of the organization.

- Provides clear objectives, necessary resources, and widespread recognition of team contributions to the organization's mission.

- Serves on executive task forces and with external groups to bridge differences of competing or conflicting groups and teams.

- Supports decisions or recommendations made by executive and managerial teams.

Behavioral Examples for Executives

Competency: **Technical Credibility**

Definition: Understands and appropriately applies principles, procedures, requirements, regulations, and policies related to specialized expertise.

Behavioral Examples for the Executive Role

- Fosters and rewards high standards for accuracy, safety, and constant improvement in all areas of the organization.

- Ensures organization builds technical capacity needed to implement strategic goals.

- Promotes an ongoing assessment of organizational technical capability and builds capability in support of strategic direction.

- Acquires necessary capital resources to implement organizational goals and objectives.

- Provides expert testimony or personal support to head of organization during Congressional/legislative testimony or meetings of other high-level organizations, resulting in positive action.

- Seeks input from others when in-depth subject matter expertise outside of own area is required.

- Encourages managers and supervisors to see that supervisory effectiveness is a needed focus in their technical credibility development.

Behavioral Examples for Executives

Competency: **Technology Management**

Definition: Keeps up to date on technological developments. Makes effective use of technology to achieve results. Ensures access to and security of technology systems.

Behavioral Examples for the Executive Role

- Allocates sufficient funds for future technology investment.

- Ensures the information technology plan for the organization supports strategic goals.

- Promotes the development of IT programs and support systems that better ensure seamless delivery of services and ease of use.

- Employs a knowledge management system that supports decision making with the right information available to the right people at the right time.

- Ensures compatibility of hardware/software within a major organization and among agencies.

- Institutes policies to improve technological capabilities in most cost-effective manner.

- Strategically and systematically plans for IT training and education across the organization, and monitors the effectiveness of this training.

- Works with CIOs to understand and plan for full range of costs relating to the acquisition and use of equipment and information technology.

Behavioral Examples for Executives

Competency: **Written Communication**

Definition: Writes in a clear, concise, organized, and convincing manner for the intended audience.

Behavioral Examples for the Executive Role

- Uses a variety of written communications, particularly within automated and networked media, to gain widespread understanding and commitment for change and action inside and outside of the organization.

- Ensures sensitive or complex written materials, program plans, or media scripts accurately communicate program policy and appropriately inform the public.

- Creates a written voice that is personal, visible, and recognizable and that inspires trust and commitment among employees and stakeholders.

- In the face of challenges to policy or strategy, writes convincingly for continued stakeholder support.

- Creates widespread ownership and commitment to the organization's policies, goals, and strategies by keeping stakeholders and employees informed.

- Edits to avoid stereotypes, region-specific metaphors and images, and innuendoes.

- Avoids humor in written documents with international audience, as humor is culture specific.

Chapter 8:
Developmental Learning Experiences

You're not going to change if you don't expose yourself to new ideas, tools, models, and skills. And you're not going to change if you don't *do* something different. I'm guessing that you are reading this guide because you seek some sort of change. The key: new knowledge and a chance to put it to use. Developmental learning experiences are designed to provide you both with the intellectual understanding of something and the ability to use that knowledge in some sort of behavior.

Most of us tend to think of formal classroom training as the primary resource for developing our skills. While classroom learning is a valuable learning resource, other avenues of learning are equally or more effective. Developmental assignments -- such as details, shadowing, and action learning projects -- are excellent means of development if the assignments are specifically structured to ensure learning occurs. A third group of learning experiences, self-directed activities, allows employees to learn independently, examples of these learning activities include taking online courses and reading books. The following pages contain explanations of various learning experiences that might be available to you.

Formal Classroom Training

The first thing most of us thing about in terms of development is formal classroom training. We've all been in the classroom; it is something familiar for us. It is the go-to modality for learning new content and getting a chance to put that knowledge to use.

Where can you get formal classroom training? You're either going to attend formal training through your employer or on your own.

Many organizations, particularly large organizations, will provide classroom leadership development opportunities. The organization may have its own training staff, or the organization might contract with outside vendors, or the organization might pay for you to attend public training sessions.

Talk with your supervisor about classroom training (and other developmental opportunities) available through your employer. If you are lucky enough to work for the federal government, the options are numerous. Many agencies have their own training facilities. The U.S. Coast Guard's Leadership Development Center, founded in 1998, is the premier leadership development center in the Department of Homeland Security and serves as a benchmark to other agencies for leadership development. It is merely one of dozens of centers of excellence focused on leadership development in the federal government. Talk to your supervisor to find out what is available in your organization.

For classroom training, don't focus on longer training opportunities. Frequently organizations will host classroom training sessions of a couple of hours to a couple of days in length. You may also find your organization offers training in a number of different stovepipes. Training might be available through a training team but also through program-specific teams (such as quality, equal opportunity, or diversity; you'd be surprised where you might find opportunities.

Your organization might also contract with outside vendors to either provide training in-house or through outside or open class offerings. One such vendor for federal, state, and local government agencies is Graduate School USA which traces its roots back to the USDA Graduate School and has been providing developmental opportunities since 1921. You can find more information at https://www.graduateschool.edu/.

In the federal government, entire agencies and sub-organizations are dedicated to providing developmental opportunities for government employees. These include the Federal Executive Institute (FEI) and the Office of Personnel Management (OPM).

And, finally, there are community resources that host developmental opportunities. Colleges, universities, and private organizations all hold classroom learning experiences. Look online for leadership courses offered by nongovernmental entities. You can also contact your local colleges and universities for information on offerings in your community.

Developmental Assignments

Developmental assignments provide opportunities to gain skills and knowledge by performing a structured task. These assignments can be either a primary source of learning (such as receiving instruction from another employee, observing someone, or working on a team project during which the team learns together) a method of putting into practice knowledge or skills you gained through another learning experience, such as taking a course or reading a book.

Details

Details last a minimum of 2 weeks (3 to 4 weeks is preferable, if you can arrange it) and can extend as long as 4 months.

A detail occurs outside of your current job description and provides opportunities to practice the skills or behaviors you listed in your development plan. The detail can be in your program area or another program area, depending on your learning goals, and should involve interacting with a group of people outside your normal work unit. This new setting not only provides you the opportunity to learn new skills and information, but also provides a fresh environment in which to try out new skills.

Shadowing

This developmental assignment is further outside your current job description than is a detail and provides opportunities to observe the skills or behaviors listed in your development plan. A shadowing assignment also provides you with an opportunity to network and view your own program from a different perspective.

Unlike a detail, a shadowing assignment is about "observing how experts perform" rather than applying new skills yourself. Shadowing is used when you want to explore a new area but do not have the skills to perform in that area. A shadowing assignment is typically a day to a week in duration and a report of what you learned is expected at the conclusion.

Rotations and cross-training

Cross-training provides opportunities for employees to acquire knowledge and skills from their coworkers. Typically, employees with similar grade levels and background experiences pair up or form small groups to teach one another the specific tasks and special knowledge needed for each of their jobs. This type of experience offers a chance to learn at little or no cost, and allows employees to fill in when others are ill or on vacation, preventing service gaps and reducing costs.

Once employees are cross-trained, rotations can be utilized to allow employees to practice and improve their new knowledge and skills. Rotations also provide employees with greater variety in work activities and a broader list of experiences to include in résumés when applying for new positions. Meet with your supervisor to discuss possible cross-training opportunities that might exist for you.

Special teams, task forces, and assignments

Another effective way to learn new skills is to serve on a special team or task force or work on a new assignment. In these learning assignments, you use your current skills in a new environment as well as learn new skills while accomplishing the assigned task.

To participate in such groups and projects, let your Supervisor know you are interested in developing your skills in a particular area. Your Supervisor can inform you when a project becomes available that would allow you to develop skills in the identified areas. Be on the lookout for such projects yourself and if they occur, request to join in that effort. When you include this type of learning activity in your Development Plan, describe the area in which you wish to develop your expertise and indicate that you hope to develop it by working on a special team or task force or by taking on a special assignment.

Action learning projects

In an action learning project, learning occurs as an employee or a group of employees addresses an actual work challenge or need. The individual or group develops a plan to address the stated need and then implements that plan, using existing knowledge and experience in a new way and building new knowledge and skills as needed for the project. Two important benefits of action learning projects are the learning that occurs naturally along the way and the satisfaction of a completed project that may help numerous employees.

Mentoring

Mentoring is a voluntary relationship in which a more-experienced employee provides advice, guidance, and support to a less-experienced employee. Often the mentor is someone who has experience in a job or task about which the protégé wants to either learn more or to which the protégé aspires. The mentor is not in the protégé's chain of command and has no supervisory authority over the protégé. Mentors help protégées clarify career goals, understand the organization, analyze strengths and developmental needs, build support networks, and deal with challenges.

Mentoring is a cost-effective way to upgrade skills, both for the mentor and the protégé. It can also support job retention, increase job satisfaction, and facilitate personal and career development. Both men- tors and protégées can use mentoring as a learning activity.

Teaching others

As contradictory as it may seem, teaching others is a learning experience. First, teaching others reinforces your own learning in the subject you are teaching— remember the adage that if you really want to learn something, you need to teach it.
Second, teaching others provides you with the opportunity to develop other competencies such as "Oral or Written Communication" and "Developing Others."

Community service

"Community service" means employees volunteering to benefit a community. Community service can be used as a learning experience if it is designed to practice a targeted competency. For example, if you took a class on public speaking in order to improve your oral communication skills, you could volunteer to speak at local community functions or schools on your area of expertise. If you were taking accounting courses as part of your plan to apply for a higher-level position in that area and your current job did not allow you to practice those skills, you could volunteer elsewhere to gain the needed experience.

Self-Directed Learning Activities

Self-directed learning activities include such experiences as taking online courses, reading, networking, and participating in forums, briefings, and seminars. In the following section, you will find a description of each of the above self-directed activities, as well as an explanation of the benefits and availability of each.

Employer-sponsored Learning Management Systems

Many large organizations have employer-sponsored learning management systems with provide online training and a way to manage the training. A learning management system might have hundred or thousands of courses available. Content providers such as Skillsoft and LinkedIn might provide professionally-produced development content. Learning opportunities delivered in learning management systems can provide a cost-effective way to get oriented to a new field of study as well as acquire in-depth knowledge and skills in a particular area of interest. Courses taken in the learning management system are generally automatically recorded in your learning history, a feature that helps you track progress toward your career goals.

Distance learning opportunities

People think distance learning is a new concept, but distance learning dates back to the 1700s, with degree programs being offered as early as the mid-1800s. Traditional forms of distance learning are still available as universities, private companies, and government agencies provide correspondence courses on many subjects. Materials for these courses could include books, cassette tapes, CDs, and DVDs.

While traditional distance learning is still available, much of today's distance learning tends to be in the form of e-learning. E-learning encompasses online courses,web-based training, audio and video podcasts, and a constant stream of new learning options.

Distance learning, including e-learning, is usually less expensive than formal classroom sessions, and is sometimes free. It is not constrained by geography and often allows more flexibility with time. One of the most popular online development portals is LinkedIn. Unless, you're a premium member, you can't take advantage of the formal learning opportunities under the LinkedIn Learning banner. Thousands of short (and longer) video vignettes are available on topic after topic. Another popular site is Udemy, an online learning platform where you can purchase by the course or with a subscription plan.

Reading

Employees often overlook reading as an inexpensive tool to increase knowledge and skills. You can also search online, visit a bookstore, or ask your mentor, supervisor, or colleagues for ideas for reading materials related to your targeted competency.

Coaching

Employees can be coached by someone inside or outside their own organization. Coaching can also be a component of a leadership course or other program helping participants put what they have learned in a class into practice on the job.

Coaches assist learning by encouraging employees they coach to reflect on their behaviors and develop goals for building their strengths and managing their weaknesses. Coaches do this by listening, asking questions, observing reactions, and asking for commitment. With a willing individual, coaching can be a powerful learning tool for developing one's full potential.

Forums, briefings, and seminars

Forums, briefings, and seminars are meetings focused on the exchange of information and ideas on policy, research, or other areas. Attending these meetings provides you with an opportunity to learn and can be a way to bring information back to a larger group of employees. In your development plan, propose to attend meetings covering a specific topic and offer to relay the information you learn to your colleagues upon your return. In additional to being great learning and teaching experiences, these meetings are good opportunities to network with others in your field or with those in a field you are exploring.

Networking

Networking is establishing a mutually beneficial relationship with other employees, customers, and people in businesses, universities, and professional organizations who can assist you in a specific goal or task. Once you have established a goal and analyzed what kind of support you need, develop a network of contacts to whom you can turn for assistance. The relationships you develop through your network- ing can work both ways, because there will be times you can assist as well as receive assistance. Finally, as you interact with the contacts in your network, those individuals will come to know your interests and may suggest potential learning opportunities (e.g., informing you about upcoming meetings or projects or inviting you to join new or existing working groups).

Assessments

Assessment instruments are used to identify strengths, personal styles, and developmental needs. Assessments can be both learning experiences as you discover more about yourself and tools to guide your development efforts. We'll discuss four assessment instruments: 360° assessments, Myers-Briggs Type Indicator, Fundamental Interpersonal Relations Orientations-Behavior (FIRO-B), and DiSC Assessment.

360° Assessment

A 360° assessment is feedback on your strengths and opportunities for improvement in various aspects, depending on what the tool is based on. Federal agencies frequently use 360° survey tools based on the leadership competencies.

A person who wants to receive 360°feedback, must identify potential raters in each of the necessary categories: supervisor, peers, employees, and customers. Usually, each rater will receive an email with a link to the survey. The results are summarized and sent to the employee. If you are conducting a 360° at work, hopefully the results come along with an offer to assist using the results development planning. You may be wondering how you can get a 360° if your employer does not offer the service. 360° survey tools are actually available online and as a part of a book purchase. Some are free. And, amazingly, some of the free ones are superb. FranklinCovey offers 360° assessment tools based on its various books, courses, and models. These are high quality, reliable and valid tools. You can find more information at https://assessments.franklincovey.com/.

The 360° Assessment should be used for development, not for personnel decisions. The results should be issued to the employee, who can then make the decision about whether to share the results.

Myers-Briggs Type Indicator (MBTI)

The MBTI will help you to understand your personality type and how your preferences impact your approach to work and your interactions with the other 15 personality types. Understanding more about your preferences in planning, in receiving and completing tasks, and in interacting with others and learning how your preferences compare with others' preferences can make your work interactions more smooth and less stressful.

The MBTI is frequently used in conjunction with other training or as part of a team development effort. Teams and work units can use the MBTI to better understand: 1) the strengths and challenges each member brings to the group; and 2) the communication and interaction preferences of each member. This information can increase communication and cooperation, which in turn, leads to higher productivity and more satisfaction within the group.

The MBTI is administered by a trained MBTI administrator using an online assessment. The administrator receives the assessment results and discusses those with the person who took the assessment. The administrator can use the results to help identify learning goals the employee can include in a development plan.

FIRO-B

This assessment identifies how you tend to behave toward others and how you want them to behave toward you. The results of the FIRO-B can help you increase self- awareness in a number of areas, including how you handle interpersonal relationships and your own social needs, how others perceive you, and how you view others.

The FIRO-B provides information along three dimensions of interpersonal needs: inclusion; control; and affection and indicates your preference in regard to two aspects of each of these areas: expressed behavior and wanted behavior.

DiSC

DiSC is a behavior assessment tool based on the DISC theory of psychologist William Moulton Marston, which centers on four different personality traits which are currently Dominance (D), Influence (I), Steadiness (S), and Conscientiousness (C).

How Do I Select the Learning Experience Best for Me?

To be considered development, the learning experiences you list in your development plan should result in changes on the job. For example, your colleagues should be able to see you taking on a new task or handling stressful situations more easily, or observe that your interactions with customers is improved or that you now make great presentations.

To apply your learning on the job requires you to combine practice with knowledge acquisition. Taking an online or in-person course or reading a book provides you with "book knowledge." To turn this passive knowledge into action, pair a learning activity in which you practice the new knowledge with a learning activity in which you acquired the knowledge. For example, if you attend a course on active listening and then practice one of the suggested actions each week, you will find you incorporate more of the actions into your behavior than if you only attend the course.

Which format of learning experiences you use for these two parts of the learning (the knowledge-gaining portion and the practicing por- tion) depends on many factors, such as the competency you are targeting, your learning style preference, Internet accessibility, and the rhythm of your workload, family obligations, or travel policies. Review the learning experiences described in this chapter, think creatively, and talk with your colleagues and supervisor for ideas on how to best use the available learning experiences to reach your development goals.

Afterward

You've read your way to the end. Or perhaps you thumbed your way here. Either way, welcome to the Afterward.

Perhaps you're thinking, "Is that all there was?" Well, yes, guess that is all there is. That's all there ever is. We are continuously assessing our environment, looking toward where we want to go, plotting a way forward, and then heading out on the journey, adjusting as we go. That's life. That's professional development.

Now, because it is simple does not mean that it is easy. The seven steps are remarkably simple. As is are the multitude of behavioral examples provided through the guide. But it's not easy. There will be innumerable obstacles in your way was you execute your way through the seven step process. I know this, as I, too, have had these obstacles land in my path.

We have a choice. We can turn around and go back down the path from whence we came. Or, we can go over, or around, or dig under. Or we can push it aside. However we do, we will deal with this boulder. Perhaps it is the bullying boss who denies you every opportunity for development under the guise of organizational necessity. Or perhaps it is the co-worker who submarines you when you are out of the office for training. Or maybe you don't have any money in your house budget for training and your organization doesn't provide. Or maybe it is the supervisor who thinks you'd make a great baker (or whatever) and you have your eye set on being a maître d'. Those are all obstacles, and they are all obstacles you can push through.

Don't let these boulder stop your progress. Identify where you want to go and get moving. One thing that might help you as you move forward is a good planning tool. I'm a big fan of paper planning and have recently been using Brendon Burchard's The High Performance Planner. It's not a traditional planner, but it's generating results for me. It might be a tool you can use.

Best of luck as you move forward. If you're not moving forward, you're stagnating, and that is not doing you, your family, your community, or your employer any good. Good leadership, demonstrating the competencies in a way that those around us can see it, is needed in every aspect of our lives. Make it so.

If you find yourself along the path and there's a big boulder in the way and you don't have anywhere to turn, and everyone with the machetes who's been helping clear the jungle foliage has faded away, and you just really want some help, reach out to me on LinkedIn, and I'll see what counsel I can provide.

A Request for Your Assistance

The meat of this guide, I believe, are the behavioral examples for each of the leadership competencies for each of the roles on the leadership role continuum. I hope you agree. I hope you also agree that these examples need to be numerous and robust. Some need some work. If you have examples you would like to share, please send them my way. Please send them via email to pastinson@gmail.com and include the subject line "LDG Behavioral Example Input."

My thanks to the following people who have provided counsel and input and behavioral examples:

Lisa Tatum
Fairfax County Department of Family Services

Rhys Thomas Andrews
DC Initiatives

Let us go forth knowing that we do not travel alone.

Appendix:
Glossary of Key Terms

360° Assessment: a self, supervisory, peer/ coworker, and a subordinate assessment tool that will rate you on tasks and competencies critical to the performance of a particular occupation.

Accountability: holds self and others accountable for measurable high-quality, timely, and cost-effective results. Determines objectives, sets priorities, and delegates work. Accepts responsibility for mistakes. Complies with established control systems and rules.

Action Learning: systematically collecting and analyzing information in collaboration with others about an actual problem or need in the workplace and taking action to resolve it. After a period of time, the group reconvenes to discuss progress and make adjustments. This cycle of action and learning repeats itself until the problem or need is satisfactorily resolved.

Behavioral Example: A behavioral example is a success indicator that shows how an employee at a particular level would demonstrate proficiency in a given competency.
For example, a supervisor looking at behavioral examples for conflict management would see "Actively involves employees and team or work unit in resolving differences over work issues" while an executive would see "Provides resources and support to managers in resolving grievance and EEO complaints that reach the executive level." Behavioral examples can be used to assess proficiency in each competency.

Building Coalitions: the ability to build coalitions internally and with other organizations, Federal agencies, State and local governments, nonprofit and private sector organizations, foreign governments, or international organizations to achieve common goals.

Business Acumen: the ability to manage human, financial, and information resources strategically.

Career Guides: an official description of a position, a list of needed competencies for that position, a list of possible positions en route to the desired position, and suggested learning experiences for developing the needed skills for the position. The information in a career guide will help you develop clearer plans for getting the experience needed to apply for a desired position.

Coaching: learning assistance given to the employee through listening, observing, and providing feedback. Coaching empowers individual employees to put forth their best efforts and develop their skills. Employees can be coached by someone from within or outside the organization. Coaching is often used to enhance or further develop knowledge and skills introduced in a classroom setting. Coaching is a collaborative relationship between a coach and an employee using discovery, goal setting, and strategic actions to realize employee growth.

Coast Guard: The United States Coast Guard is America's fifth and smallest military service. It is that small core around which the Navy forms in time of war. The Coast Guard is a fantastic organization in which to develop leadership competencies. You can serve with the Coast Guard as a military member (both active duty and reserve), a civilian employee as a civil servant, or as a volunteer through the Coast Guard Auxiliary. Don't delay; develop your leadership competencies in the U.S. Coast Guard!

Competency: an observable, measurable pattern of knowledge, skills, abilities, and characteristics that can be measured against agreed- upon standards an individual needs for effective or superior job performance, which can be improved by means of learning and practice.

Conflict Management: encourages creative tension and differences of opinions. Anticipates and takes steps to prevent counter-productive confrontations. Manages and resolves conflicts and disagreements in a constructive manner.

Continual Learning: assesses and recognizes own strengths and weaknesses; pursues self- development.

Creativity and Innovation: develops new insights into situations. Questions conventional approaches. Encourages new ideas and innovations. Designs and implements new or cutting-edge programs/processes.

Cultural Transformation: the process of creating a workplace where all employees and customers are treated with dignity and respect, and provided the opportunity for success.

Customer Service: anticipates and meets the needs of both internal and external customers. Delivers high-quality products and services; is committed to continuous improvement.

Decisiveness: makes effective and timely decisions, even when data are limited or solutions produce unpleasant consequences. Perceives the impact and implications of decisions.

Detail: an assignment to another office or organization, which may vary in length from a few weeks to several months, as is the case with temporary duty assignments overseas. Employees may be detailed to other units within APHIS, to other parts of APHIS, to other Federal agencies, or, under the Intergovernmental Personnel Act, to city, county, or State government, Indian Tribal Governments, academic institutions, or approved nonprofit organizations.

Developing Others: ability of others to perform and contribute to the organization by providing ongoing feedback and by providing opportunities to learn through formal and informal methods.

Development Plan (also known as IDP): a written plan for developing necessary skills, knowledge, and abilities through appropriate training and developmental assignments. The plan reflects the developmental needs and career goals of the individual employee and is created through discussions and agreements between the employee and his/ her Supervisor. (See Learning contract and/or IDP.)

DiSC Assessment: DiSC is a behavior assessment tool based on the DISC theory of psychologist William Moulton Marston, which centers on four different personality traits which are currently Dominance (D), Influence (I), Steadiness (S), and Conscientiousness (C).

E-Learning: a wide set of applications and processes such as Web-based learning, computer-based learning, virtual classrooms, and digital collaboration. It includes the delivery of content via the Internet, intranet/extranet (LAN/WAN), audio- and videotape, satellite broadcast, interactive TV, CD-ROM, and instant messaging.

Entrepreneurship: Positions the organization for future success by identifying new opportunities. Builds the organization by developing or improving products or services. Takes calculated risks to accomplish organizational objectives.

Executive Core Qualifications (ECQs): established by the Office of Personnel Management (OPM), defines the competencies and characteristics needed to build a Federal corporate culture that drives for results, serves customers, and builds successful teams and coalitions within and outside the organization. The ECQs are required for entry into the Senior Executive Service (SES) and are used by USDA and APHIS in selection, performance management, and leadership development for Manager and Executive positions. They also provide the framework for the APHIS Leadership Roadmap. The five ECQs, under which all the leadership competencies are grouped, are: 1) Leading Change; 2) Leading People; 3) Results Driven; 4) Business Acumen; and 5) Building Coalitions and Communication.

External Awareness: understands and keeps up-to-date on local, national, and international policies and trends that affect the organization and shape stakeholders' views. Is aware of the organization's impact on the external environment.

Financial Management: understands the organization's financial processes. Prepares, justifies, and administers the program budget. Oversees procurement and contracting to achieve desired results. Monitors expenditures and uses cost-benefit thinking to set priorities.

Flexibility: open to change and new information; rapidly adapts to new information, changing conditions, or unexpected obstacles.

Fundamental Competencies: the foundation for success in all management and leadership positions, and are expected of all employees.

FIRO-B: Fundamental Interpersonal Relations Orientations-Behavior; behavioral assessment.

Human Capital Management: builds and manages workforce based on organizational goals, budget considerations, and staffing needs. Ensures employees are appropriately recruited, selected, appraised, and rewarded. Takes action to address performance problems. Manages a multi-sector workforce and a variety of work situations.

Individual Development Plan (also knowns as a Development Plan): a written plan for developing necessary skills, knowledge, and abilities through appropriate training and developmental assignments. The plan reflects the developmental needs and career goals of the individual employee and is created through discussions and agreements between the employee and his/her Supervisor. (See also "development plan.")

Influencing and Negotiating: persuades others; builds consensus through give and take. Gains cooperation from others to obtain information and accomplish goals.

Integrity and Honesty: behaves in an honest, fair, and ethical manner; shows consistency in words and actions. Creates a culture fostering high standards of ethics.

Interpersonal Skills: treats others with courtesy, sensitivity, and respect. Considers and responds appropriately to the needs and feelings of different people in different situations.

Job Rotations: permanent or temporary appointments to new positions and planned to stretch and challenge employees, as well as to broaden their understanding across different business processes of the organization.

Leadership: has many definitions, and the common themes that appear in them are: openness to change; ability to visualize the future, be guided by it and communicate it powerfully to others; entrust the mission to others; display commitment through action; bring out the best in others; and encourage followers. Those who want to become good leaders can read this Guide and work through the seven-step model which provides behavioral examples that correspond to each competency and allows for building a plan for developmental activities that might include courses, mentoring, coaching, rotational assignments, and self-development.

Leadership Competency: an observable, measurable pattern of knowledge, skills, abili- ties, or characteristics that an individual needs for effective superior performance in a leadership position. A leadership competency can be measured against agreed-upon standards and can be improved by means of learning and practice.

Leading Change: the ability to bring about strategic change, both within and outside the organization, to meet organizational goals. Inherent to Leading Change is the ability to establish an organizational vision and to implement it in a continuously changing environment.

Leading People: the ability to lead people toward meeting the organization's vision, mis- sion, and goals. Inherent to "Leading People" is the ability to provide an inclusive workplace fostering the development of others, facilitates cooperation and teamwork, and supports constructive resolution of conflicts.

Learning: covers all our efforts to adapt, absorb, understand, and respond to the world around us. Learning happens on the job every day and entails adapting for the survival and well-being of individuals as well as organizations. Types of learning include:

- *Formal learning* encompasses all traditional training in structured courses, classrooms, and formal development programs.
- *Informal learning* takes place in the informal processes of everyday work. Most learning occurs informally rather than through formal training or education.
- *Individual learning* is the ability of individuals to experience personal growth in the world around them.
- *Organizational learning* is the ability of an organization to gain insight and understanding from experience. Groups and organizations adapt, grow, and change to shape their future course.

Learning Contract (sometimes known as a development plan): a written plan for developing necessary skills, knowledge, and abilities through appropriate training and developmental assignments. The plan reflects the developmental needs and career goals of the individual employee and is created through discussions and agreements between the employee and his/her Supervisor.

Learning Experiences: activities designed to develop or enhance specific competencies and abilities, such as formal classroom training, self-directed activities, and developmental assignments. Another commonly used term is "developmental activities."

Leveraging Diversity: fosters an inclusive workplace where diversity and individual differences are valued and leveraged to achieve the vision and mission of the organization.

Management: getting work done through others by using planning, organizing, implementing, and evaluation skills.

Mentor: the more-experienced employee in a mentoring relationship.

Mentoring: a voluntary relationship whereby more-experienced employee, provides advice, guidance, and support to a less-experienced employee and assists the employee in career development. The mentor is not in the individual's chain of command and has no Supervisory authority over the person being mentored. Mentors help employees clarify career goals, understand the organization, analyze strengths and developmental needs, build support net- works, and deal with challenges. Mentoring programs may be formal or informal and done in a variety of ways, even over the Internet.

MBTI: Myers-Briggs Type Indicator; behavioral assessment

Networking: building effective lateral or peer relationships where the parties share information and, as a result, often have greater learning and increased opportunities for success.

Oral Communication: makes clear and convincing oral presentations to individuals and groups. Listens effectively. Clarifies information as needed. Facilitates open communication.

Partnering: develops networks and builds alliances. Collaborates across boundaries to build strategic relationships and achieve common goals.

Political Savvy: identifies the internal and external politics that impact the work of the organization. Perceives organizational and political reality and acts accordingly.

Problem Solving: identifies and analyzes problems. Weighs relevance and accuracy of information. Generates and evaluates alternative solutions; makes recommendations.

Protégé: employee receiving mentoring. Another word commonly used instead of protégé is mentee.

Public Service Motivation: shows a commitment to serve the public; relates to government employees. Ensures that actions meet public needs. Aligns organizational objectives and practices with public interests.

Resilience: deals effectively with pressure. Remains optimistic and persistent even under adversity; recovers quickly from setbacks.

Results driven: the ability to meet organizational goals and customer expectations. Inherent to Results Driven is the ability to make decisions producing high-quality results by applying technical knowledge, analyzing problems, and calculating risks.

Self-Development (or self-directed activities): a collection of techniques and approaches for individuals to manage their own process of learning. They include self-analysis of competencies and interests, personal Development Plans, Learning Contracts, learning logs, reading lists, involvement in professional organizations, networks, attending demonstrations at other organizations, and participating on inter- agency committees.

SES: Senior Executive Service. Members of the Senior Executive Service lead government agencies with political appointees and, in some agencies, senior, flag-level uniformed personnel. SES are most frequently career civil servants who have worked their way through the leadership role continuum to an executive role.

Shadowing: a developmental assignment in which an employee accompanies an experienced person as they carry out all of his/her professional activities during a designated period of time, (e.g., one week). This provides the employee with a detailed "snapshot" of a successful leader, including the nature of his/ her responsibilities and interaction with others.

Special Assignments: tasks or projects given as learning and development experiences. They can be specifically designed to offer opportunities to explore new areas and learn new skills.

Strategic Thinking: formulates objectives and priorities, and implements plans consistent with the long-term interests of the organization in a global environment. Capitalizes on opportunities and manages risks.

Team Building: inspires and fosters team commitment, spirit, pride, and trust. Facilitates cooperation and motivates team members to accomplish group goals.

Technical Credibility: understands and appropriately applies principles, procedures, requirements, regulations, and policies related to specialized expertise.

Technology Management: keeps up to date on technological developments; makes effective use of technology to achieve results. Ensures access to and security of technology systems.

Training: instructor-led (often in a controlled classroom environment), on-the- job, or technology-based structured content which uses various methodologies to improve current or future performance.

Vision: takes a long-term view and builds a shared vision with others; acts as a catalyst for organizational change. Influences others to translate vision into action.

Webinar: (short for Web-based seminar) a presentation, lecture, workshop, or seminar that is transmitted over the Internet. A key feature of a webinar is its interactive elements -- the ability to give, receive, and discuss information. Contrast with webcast, in which the data transmission is one way and does not allow interaction between the presenter and the audience.

Written Communication: writes in a clear, concise, organized, and convincing manner for the intended audience.

About the Editor

 For more than two decades, Peter Stinson served with the United States Coast Guard as a civil servant focused on improving individual and organizational performance. A graduate of Trinity College, Hartford, Peter earned master's degrees from George Mason University and the Naval War College. He now writes and consults from his home in Fairfax, Virginia. You can find Peter's LinkedIn profile at https://www.linkedin.com/in/pastinson/. Feel free to reach out and connect.

===========
Deer Hollow Way
Fairfax, Virginia
===========

www.ingramcontent.com/pod-product-compliance
Lightning Source LLC
Chambersburg PA
CBHW060834170526
45158CB00001B/164